Law Firm Recruitment in Canada:

Job Search Advice for Law Students and Associates

Wendy Griesdorf

160201

IRWIN
LAW

Law Firm Recruitment in Canada: Job Search Advice for Law Students and Associates
© Irwin Law Inc., 2004

Published in 2004 by

Irwin Law
347 Bay Street
Suite 501
Toronto, Ontario
M5H 2R7

www.irwinlaw.com

ISBN: 1-55221-095-2

Library and Archives Canada Cataloguing in Publication

Griesdorf, Wendy
    Law firm recruitment in Canada : job search advice for law students and associates / Wendy Griesdorf.

ISBN 1-55221-095-2

    1. Lawyers—Employment—Canada. 2. Law—Vocational guidance—Canada. 3. Job hunting—Canada. I. Title.

KE330.G75 2004   340'.023'73   C2004-904984-4
KF297.G75 2004

The publisher acknowledges the financial support of the Government of Canada through the Book Publishing Industry Development Program (BPIDP) for its publishing activities.

Printed and bound in Canada.

1 2 3 4 5   08 07 06 05 04

Table of Contents

Preface

This book is based on my experiences as an Ontario lawyer, conversations I have had with law firm recruiters across Canada, comments from law students, and lectures I gave and advice I provided while I was Director of Career Services at Osgoode Hall Law School from 2001 to 2003. The book is aims to demystify law firm recruitment and help Canadian law students and associates, primarily those who intend to practise in common law jurisdictions, in their job searches.

Pursuing a summer, articling, or associate position is similar to working on a file as a lawyer. First, written advocacy is required for your resumé and cover letter and oral advocacy is required for your interview. Second, you must research your potential employers in much the same way as you will one day research the law for a client. Third, there are recruitment rules that function in a manner that is similar to statutory regulations. If you do not adhere to recruitment rules, you will almost certainly run into significant roadblocks. And fourth, the networking you will need to do in the course of your job search is much like a series of interlocutory motions. Although interlocutory motions sometimes seem like time-consuming distractions, they can enable you to accomplish your client's goals, just as networking can help you to achieve your goal of finding a job.

To continue the analogy, when you begin to form your career plan, you ought to start with the equivalent of an initial client interview. In other words, you should begin by interviewing yourself in the manner of a lawyer interviewing a client. The purpose of this self-interview is to better understand your values and your short and long-term goals. Ask yourself where you want to be next year, and where you want to be five years from now. A good lawyer never pursues a client's case without meeting with the client first in order to ascertain the client's objectives. The lawyer will have several more meetings of this nature with the client as the file evolves. Students go through a similar process when developing their personal career file.

In addition to providing advice on the recruitment process, the purpose of this book is to help the student to develop a better understanding of his or her career preferences and work ethic. A good job for one student may not be a good job for another student. This statement may sound like a truism, but it is worth remembering. It is the responsibility of each student to understand, and to steadfastly pursue, his or her personal goals. The strength needed to do so is comparable to the fortitude of a good lawyer who is unwavering in his or her support of a client's position, sometimes in the face of extraordinary opposition. Be sure to practise this sort of resolve now and stay true to your goals. Deciding on your goals and finding the right career path is not always an easy task. It may help to consider the paths that other students have taken. Law students love statistics and law schools are increasingly eager to display their graduates' career destinations on websites. Although an overview of general trends may be informative, the figures can be misleading. It is important to remember that statistics do not provide you with information about yourself. They are an indication of group behaviour and cannot be used to determine the potential behaviour of individuals.

That said, according to statistics, every year most Canadian law school graduates article in a private practice environment (that is, in a law firm), remain in the province of their law school, and switch their jobs at least once within the first five years of being called to the Bar. Increasing opportunities in government and social justice make these areas the next most popular destinations for law school graduates. US recruitment of Canadian law students, which increased in the late 1990s, affects only a small percentage of a law school's graduating class and a just a tiny percentage of the Canadian graduating law student population overall.

Because it is becoming more common for lawyers to change their jobs and career paths in the early stages of their careers, the advice in this book is designed to be helpful to new lawyers as well as law students. New lawyers will find useful information that will help them in their job searches after they are called to the Bar. The personal workbook on pages 93–150 will assist both law students and new lawyers in outlining their ideas and plans and, at the same time, help them to establish a foundation upon which to build successful and satisfying careers. Some readers may find it helpful to make use of the workbook during meetings with their career services office, while others may wish to keep their notes private.

The personal workbook is designed to allow you to identify your shifting values and interests. When you begin to practise law, you will grow to better understand yourself and your values, and you will come to realize that the *self* is never a static entity. Your values and beliefs are subject to change when you encounter new experiences and learn new information. What is important to you today may not be important to you in ten years. A transformation of this nature does not necessarily mean that you have abandoned your original goals, but rather that the point of reference upon which your values and beliefs are based has shifted. A good career plan will be flexible and open to this type of change.

As a Canadian law student, you are now a part of the law profession. Remember, your professional reputation begins when you enter, not when you exit, law school. Your fellow classmates are going to be your colleagues for life. They will remember you and you will remember them. In addition, the lawyers who interview you when you are a student will remember you in the years to come, just as you will remember meeting them. Law school is the ideal time for you to begin to develop your professional reputation. While you are in law school you will start to build a network of associates. These associates will be a valuable asset to you throughout your career. The relationships you form with others in your profession should be built slowly and with discretion. As my grandfather once wisely said, "never burn bridges." The people you meet today may prove to be resources for you, and you for them, a decade from now. As long as you are discreet and professional, the people you encounter in law school will regard you highly in the years to come.

I would like to thank Stacey Stevens for her very hard work in transcribing many hours of my lectures and for enduring my idiosyncratic style. I would also like to thank Kandirra Wilson, who generously read drafts of this book on her own time and provided useful comments and ideas. Finally, I wish to thank Catherine Hatt for editing the manuscript and my publisher, Jeffrey Miller, for his support and encouragement.

Wendy Griesdorf

one: **Preparation**

Resumés and Cover Letters[1]

Your entire law firm application, especially the cover letter, reveals the high quality of work you will do for a firm once you are a lawyer. This is true for job searches in every city and in every country. Treat the application stage as if it were your first assignment at the office. Your application is the firm's first, and best, opportunity to see whether you write well, whether you complete assignments in a timely manner, whether you can proofread your own work, and whether you can develop an effective and compelling narrative about who you are and why you have applied for the job.

Strive for a standard of perfection when working on your applications. You should spend as much time working on your applications as you would spend on a law school course. Start by taking some time to think about yourself and who you are. Your cover letter should address why you should be hired over the six hundred other applicants.

When you review your letter, pretend that you are the recruiter. Have you indicated why you want to work at the firm and why you should be hired over everyone else? In

---

1   Refer to the "Sample Resumé and Analysis" and the "Sample Cover Letter and Analysis" on
    pages 93–102 for more detail.

your letter, you should strategically pick and emphasize facts about yourself that will help you to get the job. Remember, everything you are going through during the application process is good training for when you are a lawyer, especially if you plan to go into private practice and deal with clients. When you are in court, you may only have five minutes to summarize the facts of your client's case. What you say, and more importantly, what you omit, is strategic.

Here are some general points about resumés and cover letters:

Presentation

1. **Printing.** Laser print your resumé and cover letter. Every Canadian law office uses laser printing and the lawyers who work in these offices are accustomed to reading laser quality printouts. It is worthwhile to go to your local copy shop or your law school library and print out your application on a laser printer.

2. **Templates.** Be consistent: use the same template for your resumé and your cover letter.

3. **Editing.** Proofread your resumé and your cover letter or, preferably, have someone else proofread them. If there are errors in either of them, a firm may lose confidence in the quality of your work and your ability to write well. If you have more than two typos or errors in your application package, you should not be surprised if a firm decides not interview you.

4. **Visual Presentation.** Create a lot of white space. The visual impact of your resumé and your cover letter is very important. The lawyers interviewing you will write on your resumé and add their comments to it. The layout of your resumé should allow interviewers the opportunity to do so easily. You will follow the same procedure when you are preparing a factum for court; allow room on the paper so that judges can write comments on your material while you are presenting your oral argument.

5. **Paper.** Do not use dark-coloured paper or patterned stationery. It is unprofessional. This is not a letter sent home to your parents from summer camp.

6. **Re:** Include a "re" line that clearly indicates the position for which you are applying. Your "re" line ensures that your application is put in front of the proper lawyer or recruiter. Law firms hire secretaries, students, associates, clerks and partners at all times and it is not uncommon for two recruitment programs to be running concurrently. If your application is inadvertently placed in the wrong pile because you were not clear as to the position for which you were applying, you will lose the opportunity to get the job, regardless of your qualifications.

7. **Delivery.** Avoid sending your resumé and cover letter by fax or e-mail unless prompted to do so by the firm. If you absolutely have to meet a deadline, go ahead, but realize that you have no control over the visual quality of your application when it goes by fax. If the law firm's fax machine or printer is running out of ink, or if there is a

partial transmission error, your material will not be legible. Consider that a resumé is seen before it is read. The visual impact of your resumé is important.

Sentences

1. **Clear Language.** Try to avoid phrases such as "please find enclosed." It is a phrase that you will see often when you are practising, but it is considered business jargon. Use phrases such as "I am enclosing" or "I have enclosed." Be as clear as possible.

2. **Brevity.** Keep your sentences and your paragraphs short. Remember, your application should not be written in the style of an academic essay. This may be your first experience with business writing. In business writing, you should be concerned with content and brevity. You must be clear and concise in your writing. Keep in mind that the lawyer reading your material may bill $250 or even $400 an hour. You do not want to waste her time. Generally, good business writing is characterized by short sentences (five to ten words) and short paragraphs (three to five sentences). Divide up your longer paragraphs. You may feel as if you are returning to a grade five level of writing. Business writing is not easy at first, especially if you are accustomed to academic writing. In the beginning, you will probably need to *edit down* your work. Eventually, it will become easier and you will find that you are able to adopt the business style when you are writing your first draft.

3. **Deliberate Wording.** Every word in your resumé and your cover letter should be there because you have chosen it; nothing should be inadvertent. It is helpful to analyze the marketing of successful commercial products to see how language can be used effectively. Nike is a good example ("Just do it"), as is Coke ("The real thing"). I am not advocating the use of slogans, but rather attempting to get you to analyze the process through which companies communicate their messages. Examine how they communicate whole concepts and build images with just a few words. Use a thesaurus. Use a dictionary. Use clear and direct words to describe what you are trying to communicate.

4. **Active Voice.** Try to avoid the passive voice; instead, use the active voice. You will generate energy in your tone and tighten up your sentences.

5. **Avoid Exaggeration.** When you write your cover letter, be sure to delete extraneous facts and descriptors. Include only what is essential about your experience and that which makes you a compelling candidate. Every word and every sentence should be informative. Every adjective should be accurate and included for a reason. Be sure to avoid exaggeration.

   Here is an example of hyperbole:

   "I am applying to your firm because you are the best in intellectual property law."

If you switch from a superlative statement to a comparative statement, the information can be conveyed without exaggeration. Here is a revised version of the sentence:

> "I am applying to your firm because it is apparent from my research that you are *among the leaders* in intellectual property law."

Shifting from the superlative to the comparative allows you to make a safer and more accurate statement. Because the comparative statement is more likely to be true than the superlative statement, the choice of a comparative statement will attest to your credibility whereas the choice of a superlative statement may undermine it. In addition, the revised version of the sentence allows you to point out that you conducted research before applying for the job.

The following sentence provides the recruiters with too much information:

> "In my office, I am among the hardest workers and I often work through weekends."

By saying, "I am among the hardest workers" and then adding, "I often work through weekends," you have made a conclusion about yourself first and then offered your evidence second. It is preferable to let the recruiters conclude on their own that you are among the hardest workers, based on the evidence you provide. In other words, you do not want to make conclusions about yourself. What you want to do is give the recruiters enough evidence about your work habits so that they can arrive at the conclusion that you are a hard worker themselves. Here is the same information, but in a better crafted sentence:

> "In my office, I frequently meet project deadlines early and often work through weekends."

Now, both halves of the sentence provide evidence of your hard work. The recruiters are able to conclude on their own that you are "among the hardest workers" without you having to say so.

6. **Strategic Use of Words.** It is important to develop a thesis about yourself and to communicate this thesis in your resumé and your cover letter. You can do so by strategically choosing the words that you use to describe yourself. One way to learn to use words strategically is to watch the news on television. The journalists who deliver the news live every day are experts in the use of language and in the concept of core messages. Analyze these journalists and consider why their techniques are so effective. Also, observe how the presenters vary their style. You will find a marked difference in their choice of words, the tempo of their speech, and the length of their sentences, depending on the subject they are discussing. The ability to strategically choose their words and to present ideas effectively allows journalists to control the way they deliver information.

Content

1. **Areas to Cover.** One recruiter at a large, full-service, national law firm explains that she looks for four areas to be addressed in a cover letter:

   1) The Position for Which You Are Applying. The position should be indicated in your "re" line and should also appear in your first sentence. If you have a specific practice interest, write, "I am particularly interested in tax," or "I am particularly interested in civil litigation." If you want a full-service firm, write, "I have not made a decision yet on my area of practice and I am interested in rotating through . . . " (insert whatever departments you are interested in).

   2) Why You Are Attracted to the Firm. Be specific. Law firms may read up to six hundred applications and they read every single word of every single one of them. This means that they are experts at identifying the template or form letter. You should research the firms to which you apply and communicate in your cover letter specifically why you are attracted to these offices.

   3) What You Can Offer the Firm. Why are you the best candidate? I will get into this in more detail later, but you have to develop a thesis about yourself: a theme. What is it that makes you more competitive than the next person? Be consistent and use words that will help to develop your core message.

   4) A Courteous Closing. Keep your closing short and polite. One or two sentences should be sufficient.

2. **Detailed Content.** If you interviewed with a firm for a summer position and you are reapplying to that firm for articling, be upfront and acknowledge that you have met with them already. These firms are very sophisticated; they keep files on you because they expect you to apply to them a number of times over the next few years, even once you are a lawyer. The second application should be a sequel to the first, not a repetition of it. State that it was a pleasure to meet the firm for summer interviews and that you look forward to meeting with the firm again during the articling process.

3. **Other Interests.** If you have the space on your resumé, you should add a section on your other interests. There are two reasons for doing so. First, you many not have enough employment experience to differentiate yourself from other applicants. The law firms understand this problem, but they still want to know more about you. They want to know a little bit about your character. Your hobbies and interests will speak to your character.

   Another reason to include your interests is that it may give you the opportunity to control the first five minutes of an interview. When you sit down at the beginning of an interview, everyone is nervous, including the interviewer. The interviewer will probably begin the interview on a lighter topic and may turn to whatever is listed in your other interests section for subject matter. By increasing the possibility of having a conversation on something that you are comfortable speaking about, you increase the possibility that the first few minutes of the interview will go smoothly for you. Also, some law firms pair up students with interviewers based on their interests (e.g., joggers with joggers, musicians with musicians).

4. **Market Your Assets.** Individuals get hired. The firms are looking for individuals. They want to hire students who are different from the average student. Aspects of your life history, academic studies, and work experience that make you different from the next student can be assets. Be sure to highlight your individuality in your application package and try to avoid making your package seem like the next student's package.

5. **Diversity.** Draw attention to your cultural background in your resumé. The goal of the law profession across Canada is have to a heterogeneous profession, in keeping with the ideals of the whole country. Your ability to speak another language or to attract a client base from another country (or from a different province) can provide a profitable opportunity for a firm, especially in a global market. You should consider your cultural background to be an asset you can offer a firm, especially if you have lived in other places.

6. **Language Accuracy.** Be accurate about the level of your language abilities. The firms may spend a portion of the interview asking you to speak in one of your listed languages. If you are only conversational in the language, place the word "conversational" beside the language indicated on your resumé. If you are fully bilingual in French and English, then list it that way. If you are currently in an introductory Urdu class, go ahead and put that down and the firm will have a lower expectation of your Urdu-speaking abilities. There is a tremendous amount of client work that needs to be conducted in a number of different countries. If you indicate that you speak the languages of these new and emerging client bases, you will make yourself more attractive to the law firms.

Preparation

1. **Research the Firms.** Visit the law firms' websites. Read *Lexpert* or *Career Verdict*, both of which are in every law school's career services office. Read the newspapers for transactions and court cases that the firms are working on. When you read recent cases in class, look for the lawyers' names below the style of cause. Find out where they work. If you are really impressed with a case, you may want to discuss it during an interview and ask if you can meet the lawyer(s) involved. You could also indicate that your reason for applying to the firm was because you admired the position taken by lawyer X on case A. You should demonstrate that you have conducted research of this nature in your cover letter. You do not have to go to great lengths; one or two sentences will likely be sufficient to establish the research you have done.

2. **Rules.** Read every word of the rules. All recruitment processes are regulated either by a provincial law society or a city bar association. In Ontario, the law society reg-

ulates each recruitment process to such an extent that it may be considered professional misconduct if you break the rules. In particular, Toronto is very strict with deadlines and periods of time in which recruitment is disallowed (known as *black-out periods*). In other big cities, such as Vancouver and Ottawa, the process is becoming more formalized. In the Atlantic provinces, recruitment is completely different from elsewhere: if you are hired for an articling position you are also offered a summer job with the firm. It is very important to read the rules for each recruitment process and to keep reading them over and over until you understand them. This preparation is the key to navigating successfully through recruitment processes. It is no different from how you will practise law.

3. **Layer the Process.** Because many of the recruitment cycles deal with a high volume of applications, especially when it comes to articling positions, pick your ten most-preferred offices and treat them differently from the next ten firms. Also, treat the firms that you have met before in another recruitment cycle in a different manner. Treat the small firms differently from the large ones. Government cover letters should also be different because you will be speaking more about your commitment to the public interest than about your personal goals.

4. **Mindset.** The process of preparing for recruitment is a bridge between being a student to being a professional. It is not like any other job that you have applied for. It is the beginning of your career. The process is as important as any course that you will take in law school. You should expect to do as much work for the application process as you would when studying for an exam, assuming of course that you want to get an A on your career. Do the research. Do the work. The amount (and quality) of work a student puts into an application affects the outcome of the job search. You must take control over the process and factor it into your schedule properly.

5. **Games vs. Strategy.** Students often speak about the application process as if it were a game. The application process is not a game, obviously. If you think that you are playing a game, so will the law firm. Start thinking about the application process in terms of *strategy*, rather than viewing it as a *game*. Everything that you did that led to your acceptance into law school was strategic. Everything that you do to get a job is also going to be strategic. If you take control over the direction of your life you will achieve your goals and career satisfaction.

Remember to be proud of your accomplishments. Remember how you felt the day you received notice of your acceptance into law school. You need to recapture this pride for the job application process. You do not want to boast, but rather to have a professional sense of pride in your accomplishments. If you have had a couple of setbacks — everyone has them, and these are usually periods during which your character matures — look at the other things that you have achieved.

All law students these days excel at performance output and often perform at a level that is far above average. There will be times when you will perform at an average or below-average level. This fluctuation is a natural part of being human. You must not fear the occasional below-average performance. If you do, you will have a difficult time in your law practice. Files will occasionally fall apart and you will not win every court case. It is what you do when that happens and how you manage to keep going that will define your character and professionalism. Recognize these rare moments in your life for what they are, learn from them, and then move on with a positive attitude.

The more information you acquire, the better off you are during the application process. The same situation will arise when you are a lawyer and your client hires you to do some work for him. Treat your own career development the same way. Keep a file on yourself. Keep notes on the offices to which you have applied. Keep samples of your cover letters so that you know you are not repeating the same cover letter when you apply next year to the same office. How you handle your career development and how you handle the application process indicates to the firms how you will handle clients. This is a good time to practise the type of lawyering style you want to develop. If you are organized and on top of things, from now through to the end of your interviews, you will make a good impression on the firms to which you apply.

two: **Interviews**

Fifty Points on Interviewing

Interviewing is always difficult, whether you are interviewing for a summer job, an articling position, or an associate position. Fortunately, the more you interview, the better at it you become. Confident law students and junior lawyers find a way to suppress any anxiety they experience during interviews. Remember, it is your job to engage the interviewer in an interesting dialogue about why you are the best candidate for the job. Avoid viewing the interview as an isolated, unnatural experience. Instead, approach the interview as if it were the beginning of a long-term relationship. Here are fifty points to help you to prepare for summer, articling, and associate interviews.

1. **Cost of Interviewing.** It costs at least $1000 in lost billable hours for a law firm to conduct a full interview with a student at their offices. This calculation is based on the cost of having two lawyers, who normally bill anywhere between $200 and $300 an hour, sit in a room with a student for a one or two hour interview. The figure also includes the preparation time spent selecting the candidates to be granted an interview, the time spent reading your material, and the follow-up meeting after

your initial meeting. The figure increases when you include cocktail parties, dinners, and, for Toronto, OCIs (on-campus interviews).

The expense means that no one gets an interview unless the firm is seriously considering hiring that person. These firms have no interest in wasting money. The large law firms in Toronto and Vancouver review between five and seven hundred applications each recruitment round. Other large law firms in big cities across Canada (e.g., Calgary and Ottawa) may review over three hundred applications each recruitment round. If you are among the fifty students to be granted an interview, it is very good news. In mid-sized legal markets (e.g., Victoria, Edmonton, Saskatoon, Winnipeg, London, Hamilton, and Halifax), firms receive between one and two hundred applications per recruitment cycle, sometimes for only one position. I have noticed that some students look at the situation in their city and conclude, "I am only one of fifty people; how can I possibly expect to get the job?" Think of it the other way around. The firm has read your material and is interested in you, so much so that it will spend $1000 to meet you.

2. **Motivation Behind the Interview.** The motivation behind the interview is that the office wants to hire you. Whenever you are asked a question that makes you feel uncomfortable or that you do not know the answer to, remember that the motivation behind the question is benevolent. The question is designed to learn more about you in order to hire you. Remember that a firm is not going to interview you unless it feels that you are a good candidate. If you are thrown by a question, try to remember the benevolent motives of the interviewers and you will find that you will improve your answer and your interview.

3. **What Firms Seek.** Remember that the firms are looking for colleagues and for people that they feel are trustworthy. Every time you answer a question, and every time you make a comment at a cocktail party, remember these two points.

4. **Scheduling Interviews.** The way you schedule your interviews depends on the recruitment process. In smaller cities, the number of offices involved in recruitment programs is usually small. If you take part in a recruitment program in a smaller city, expect to be granted two or three interviews at the most. In larger cities, with formal recruitment programs, you will likely be granted a large number of interviews. Be realistic when setting up your interviewing schedule. It is reasonable to accept interviews with six or seven firms in a given cycle. Remember, although the interview period in larger cities is referred to as *interview week*, most of the interviews take place within about two or three days. The rest of the week is spent returning to law firms for second interviews and attending cocktail parties and other related events.

With respect to OCIs for summer jobs, there is quite a difference between the number of interviews you should accept for on-campus interviews (OCIs) and the number of interviews you should accept for the subsequent in-firm interview round.

Although the law firms encourage you to interview with as many offices as possible, you need to be wary of interview fatigue. Accepting fifteen or seventeen interviews for OCIs does not guarantee a student a job. In fact, doing so can backfire. You may discover that you lack the endurance to take part in such a large number of interviews in one or two day period (depending on your school's program). Most career services offices will suggest that you interview with no more than fifteen firms during OCIs (over one or two days). They also suggest that you accept no more than seven interviews during the in-firm interview round (over two and a half days). Following this advice will give you a good sampling of the firms without tiring you out or overwhelming you with too much information in a short period of time.

When it comes to interviewing, quantity and quality are different things. Consider that students with fewer interviews will have more time to focus on their firms and will not have to expend all their energy attempting to deal with a hectic interviewing schedule. Another way to look at it is to ask yourself, "how many exams would I like to write in one day?" Your success depends on the quality of your interviews and not the quantity.

In both large and small cities, you may be asked what other firms you are interviewing with. You should be prepared to answer this question. Law firms are accustomed to friendly competition and there is no reason to keep your interviews a secret. If you do, the firm may become suspicious as to why you would want to keep something secret from them. Some firms, however, will not ask you who else you are meeting. In these cases, it may be indiscreet to offer this information.

5. **Interview Fatigue.** Be aware of interview fatigue. It can be detrimental to your ability to interview effectively. You need to keep in mind that you may have no control over your schedule, depending on the recruitment program and the city in which you are conducting your job search. You have to understand your own physiology and be prepared for interview fatigue. Third-year students, who have gone through a variety of recruitment programs, generally recommend that you interview with no more than three or four firms a day, unless you are participating in an intensive interviewing process such as OCIs.

6. **Adapt Your Interview Style.** As you move through your set of interviews, learn from your mistakes and improve on your technique. Because of the compressed schedule for summer and articling interviews in some cities, this improvement will require rapid learning. In Ottawa, Toronto, Calgary, and Vancouver, the interviews take place over a period of about three days in each city and some cities' recruitment periods overlap. Be sure to reflect on the whole process once you are completely done.

7. **Space Your Interviews.** Most interviews take approximately an hour and a half. If your interviews are within walking distance of one another, it is a good idea to allocate about two hours for each interview. Remember, after an interview, you will

need time to go to the washroom, grab some juice, deal with the elevators, and find the next firm. You might also need those few extra minutes if you get lost in the maze of office towers in larger cities. Allowing yourself extra time will also give you some leeway if a firm takes longer than an hour and a half to interview you.

If you are driving between interviews, consider booking one interview in the morning and one in the afternoon. Try not to rush from one interview to another and leave plenty of time so that you can collect your thoughts and enter each interview calmly. If you realize you are going to be late for an interview, telephone the firm right away and give them your new time of arrival. When you arrive for the interview, apologize for your tardiness and for putting them off their schedule, but avoid belabouring your lateness. For interviews that you must fly to, remember to factor jet lag into your schedule (e.g., when flying from Toronto to Vancouver). Be sure to leave enough time for delays that you cannot control, such as late planes or bad weather.

8. **Interview Notes.** Leave yourself some time after each interview so that you can take notes. If you go immediately from one interview to the next, you will find yourself rapidly getting confused about who said what. Large law firm interviews are a layered process. You may think that you are going to one interview with a firm, but in reality it may really be three interviews because you are moved from office to office, meeting different lawyers each time. These experiences can be overwhelming. Give yourself time before you have to go to the next firm. Regain your focus and digest the events of the previous interview.

9. **Good Signs.** If you are invited back for another interview, if you are asked if you will stay for a firm tour, or if you are invited to a meal, the firm is probably very interested in you. If you turn these opportunities down because you have another interview, be prepared for the consequences. This is another reason why you should have as few interviews as necessary. You should keep extra space in your schedule in case a firm that you really like invites you back for a second interview.

10. **Hotel Rooms.** In large cities with compressed interview schedules, some students get together and rent a hotel room in the downtown core for the day. They can relax in the room or maybe change their clothes before the next round of interviews. Sharing the cost of a hotel room, located in close proximity to your interviews, may serve your purposes better than staying at your uncle's house in the suburbs or traveling great distances within your own city.

11. **Communicate Your Schedule.** Communicating your schedule to the interviewers is absolutely essential. If you go into an interview at 10:00 a.m., you can tell the person at the beginning that you have another interview at noon. The end of the interview is a very important time and you do not want to rush the closing. If it is 11:30 a.m. and you are still in the interview, you can remind them, "I have a noon appointment and need to leave in about fifteen minutes," in order to leave yourself enough

time to get to the next interview. You should not cancel, or be late for, your next interview. It is unprofessional for a firm to try to encourage you to cancel or reschedule your other interviews. It is important that your interviewers see that you are able to manage your schedule and that you respect the other firms. This is part of the interviewers' evaluation of your suitability to become a member of their firm.

12. **Spend Time Alone.** Remember to spend a lot of time alone during your interview days. You will be physically exhausted, especially in compressed recruitment programs in which you interview over a couple of days and then have only twenty-four hours to make a decision. You will also be mentally exhausted by the amount of information that you receive. Finally, you will be emotionally exhausted because you are required to talk about yourself the whole time. It is a high-energy output process.

To make things more difficult, in this tired state you will have to make very important decisions about the direction your law career will take over the next couple of years. Time spent alone is very important. Remember what your values are and remember what is important to you. Do not get caught up in what everyone else is saying about the firms. Try to see through what the firms are saying in order to market themselves when you are attempting to determine whether they are a true match for your values. Stay true to your values when you are making these decisions or you will be unhappy at your job.

13. **Attend Career Services Seminars.** If your career services office or articling committee is conducting sessions on interviewing skills or other preparatory sessions, attend these seminars. If recruiters from various firms are coming to speak, it makes sense for you to go and see them, particularly if you plan on meeting these recruiters in an interview in the future. Even attend sessions that focus on a city that is different from the one in which you are conducting your job search. For the most part, the advice is the same for cities that are similar in size. You will probably find that the advice for Calgary, Vancouver, and even Toronto is similar. Likewise, you may find that the advice for Nanaimo, Lethbridge, and Barrie is similar.

14. **Firm Research.** Read articles about the firms. Go into Quicklaw and review the cases that lawyers at the firm have argued on areas of law that are important to you. Try to locate more information about the firm in the library, or on the internet, and build on what you knew about the firm at the application stage. You should aim to deepen your understanding of the firm once you know that you have an interview with them.

15. **Know Your Resumé.** Have an intimate knowledge of what you have written in your resumé. Make sure you remember the papers you have written, and take the time to read over your cover letter. Your familiarity with the material is important because you may have made a comment in your cover letter that is not in your resumé. The interviewer may pick up on the discrepancy and question you on it. Be prepared to

answer any questions relating to the content of your resumé, both good and bad. You may have been fired from a job or you may have had a personal conflict with a fellow employee. Be prepared to answer questions about these events in a positive and professional manner.

16. **Know the Rules.** It is very important that you know what your rights and restrictions are through the interview process and how the process works. If someone is encouraging you to deviate from the process, you should understand the implications of what the firm is suggesting and question them on it. In most cases, deviation from the rules is inadvertent, but every year there are a few offices that intentionally breach the rules. In such cases, you need to understand what they are saying to you. If they are deviating from the recruitment rules, it is a serious matter and your career services office should know about it. The various rules for each city and province are there for your best interests, both as an individual, and collectively as a student body. Read all of the rules and seek to understand them the way you would seek to understand a set of rules for an exam.

17. **Know Why You Went to Law School.** Understand your reasons for going to law school and how your experiences there have altered your thoughts and preferences. Have a self-conscious understanding of yourself. Understand where you are on the map that sets out your career path. It will help you speak coherently and deliver a complete and a consistent message about who you are. It is almost guaranteed that you will be asked this question.

18. **Know Why You Applied to the Firm.** This point is similar to point 17 and, again, another guaranteed question. Make sure that you understand why you applied to a particular firm. You must indicate to the firm that you really have a sense of why you are there and why you have selected them (beyond the salary and tuition bonus). Be prepared to communicate this information in a manner that demonstrates that you are a competitive candidate.

19. **Speak in Full Sentences.** Practise speaking in full sentences now. Drop all of the jargon that you are used to using with your friends. Changing your speech patterns is not the type of thing that you can decide to do the weekend before your interviews. You really have to build up to it, so you should start now. You must be able to speak and present yourself intelligently during any professional interview.

20. **Be Knowledgeable About Current Events.** Read the newspapers. Be current with current events. Find a way to speak neutrally about political events. There is a way to do it. It is something you will do with clients before meetings and with your colleagues at the coffee machine. The expectation in the law profession is that you are an informed, intelligent person, and you must live up to that expectation. Sometimes there is a bit of a learning curve, so work on it now.

21. **Be Able to Summarize Your Portfolio.** Make sure you can summarize aspects of your portfolio in about two or three sentences. You ought to be able to deliver concise, consistent messages, especially concerning the major papers you wrote during your undergraduate studies and in law school. If you wrote sixty pages on a topic, you may find it difficult to explain what you said in three sentences. Review your papers and practise summarizing now. Young nephews, nieces, or children can make a good practice audience. If you can keep their attention during a two-sentence description of what your lab experiment was about, then you are off to a good start.

22. **Dress Code.** Consider watching television as part of your interview preparation. Of course, I mean certain types of television. Journalists are professionals who are required to wear business clothes to work everyday. If you examine a range of journalists and their guests on television news shows, you will see how people dress in a professional business context.

Should you wear something different to the cocktail party? No. First, there is a practical component. You may finish an interview at 5:00 p.m. and then go straight to the reception at 5:30 p.m. There is no time (or place) to change your clothes. Also, these receptions are not really parties. The lawyers will come straight from their offices and they will be dressed in their regular work clothes. It may be strategic to wear what you wore to the interview to the cocktail party as well. If you wore a red blazer at the interview (women) or a red tie (men), then keep it on because your interviewer may be looking for the student in red that he met in the morning interview.

23. **Choose Comfortable Clothing.** Be sure that you are comfortable in your clothing and try not to fiddle with it during the interview. Also, try not to touch your hair during the interview. If you have a beard and decide to shave it off, you should shave it off a week before the interview, rather than the night before. If you shave your beard the night before your interview, you may find that your face stings or itches during your interview. Finally, do not touch your face during the interview.

Remember to test your clothing. Try on the outfit you are going to wear to your interviews a few days beforehand. Put a chair in front a full-length mirror, sit on the chair, and look at yourself in the mirror. During your interviews, the table may be pushed off to the side so you should know what the lawyers are going to see when you sit down. Women who wear skirts above the knee and men who wear short socks should think twice about doing so during their interviews. Men who wear short socks will be surprised to see that they lose eight inches in the pant leg when they sit down. Men should opt for dress socks or knee-length socks. Women should opt for pants or a skirt that falls to the knee (or below the knee) when they are standing.

24. **Reveal Your Professional Side.** What you communicate during the interview is indicative of the professional that you are becoming. It is impossible for an interviewer to learn everything about you as a person in an interview. You are very complicated and complex; no one is trying to understand you completely in twenty minutes or even two hours. All the interviewers need to understand is your professional side and your work ethic; therefore, you should highlight these aspects of your personality during the interview. It is not be uncommon to feel that the interviewers did not really get to know you after an interview.

25. Behave Like a Colleague. Another way to prepare yourself is to behave as if you are already a colleague of the interviewers during the interview.

26. The Twenty-Minute Interview. If your law school runs an on-campus interview program for summer jobs with large law firms in Toronto or New York, you need to prepare for the shorter, pre-screening interview. Many people complain that a twenty-minute interview is too short (twenty minutes is the maximum time allowed for most OCIs), but you must remember that a great deal can be accomplished in twenty minutes. There is a tremendous amount of time in an OCI to communicate a lot of information, if you are well prepared. If an entire episode of a television sitcom can unfold in twenty-three minutes, you have enough time to communicate what you need to make known during an OCI.

27. Prepare for Your Own Nervousness. The nervousness you experience during an interview is similar to the nervousness you experience at the beginning of an exam. This nervousness often manifests itself in an adrenalin rush. Adrenalin can make the ears ring or make the hands sweat. By now, you should be familiar with the sensation and know how your body reacts to it. If you suspect that an adrenalin rush is going to occur, remember to calm down and ride it through. If the first two minutes of the interview are not going well because you are too nervous, do not jump to the conclusion that the rest of the interview will be a write off. You will find, as time passes, that your body will absorb the rush and you will return to a more normal state. Keep breathing. It will help push the adrenalin through your body.

28. Eye Contact. Try to maintain as much eye contact as is natural for you and is reasonable during the interview. Eye contact is a sign of warmth and friendliness in our culture. You need to make eye contact and smile *at least* at the beginning and at the end of the interview. You may forget to do so, so take a note of it and practise now. Also, be aware of the impact of eye contact in relation to cross-cultural differences. This advice is relevant to students from a different culture and to students who meet with an interviewer who is from a different culture.

29. Stay Alert and Interested. Try to stay alert and interested during the interview. A lack of alertness indicates interview fatigue. Focus your attention in the way you would for an athletic event or an exam. Drink something with caffeine if necessary. If you find yourself getting tired, concentrate on maintaining eye contact. The act of doing so may wake you up a bit.

30. **Never Speak Badly of Others.** Never say negative things about another student or another firm and do not gossip about professors. Remember the old-fashioned saying, "if you do not have anything nice to say about someone do not say anything at all." You should not allow your interview to be devoted to unpleasant conversations. By association, the negativity will be applied to you. This is your interview and you should try to steer everything into a positive conversation. Remember, your goal is to send a positive message to the firms.

31. **Drink Colourless Drinks.** If you are offered something to drink, either during an interview, at a reception, or at a meal, consider asking for a colourless drink. This includes water, Perrier, ginger ale, white wine, beer, etc. Should you accidentally spill your drink on your clothes, a colourless drink will not ruin your outfit. Not having to worry about spilling red wine or cola may ease some of the tension for you.

32. **Confidence vs. Arrogance.** There is a difference between confidence and arrogance. It is very important to be confident and proud of your accomplishments. You should be proud that you are in law school. You probably have several laudable accomplishments in your portfolio already. You should be able to speak very confidently about what you achieved prior to and during law school.

    Arrogance occurs when you go one step further and you talk about yourself in terms that do not match the reality of your achievements. I want to stress the importance of keeping your confidence tailored exactly to your level of accomplishment. Do not overstate your achievements or you will run the risk of undermining them.

33. **Honesty and Integrity.** Third-year students often speak about honesty and integrity, especially those who get hired. They report that they felt that they were being very true to who they were during their successful interviews and that they did not jeopardize their integrity in order to get the job.

    You have to be honest and you have to have integrity. These attributes are connected and speak to your moral character and your level of professionalism. You must have a sense of who you are and you must be able to articulate this sense of yourself. For example, let us say that you studied grade ten piano, but you did not take the conservatory exam. If you represent yourself inaccurately, it calls to question every other statement you made in your resumé. Remember, law firm interviewers are often expert cross-examiners. If you inflate one attribute, they will not know what to trust and what to distrust. Be completely accurate and demonstrate integrity throughout the whole application and interview process.

    To achieve this accuracy, temporarily adopt a mild paranoia. Pretend that all of the statements that you make in all of your different interviews will be collected by someone and read from start to finish. If this were to happen, you would have to take great care not to mislead anyone and your statements would have to be consistent. You should consider this to be the beginning of your professional life; as a lawyer, you can never mislead anyone. You have a higher onus placed on you for honesty than a member of the general public. You cannot tell more than one firm that they are your favourite firm; however, you can tell more than one firm that you have a preference for them. You have to watch what you say. The recruiters are often friends with one another and may have lunch together after the interviews are over.

34. **Communicate Your Preferences.** Communicate that you have a preference for the firm if you have one; the firms like to hear it. The caveat is that your statement must be honest and accurate (see point 33 above). If you indicate that you favour the firm, you will help the firm to distinguish candidates that are truly interested in the firm from candidates who are just applying for every job posting.

35. **Treat Everyone Equally.** Do not assume that that the new associate is any different from a partner when you are being interviewed. Treat everyone with respect, especially the receptionist who sees each candidate when he or she enters the office and may offer comments to the hiring committee. Everyone has a role to play. You would be surprised to learn to whom the recruitment team turns for an opinion on you.

36. **Everything Is Evaluated.** Disregard any statements along the lines of "do not worry, this is off the record." If someone prompts you in this way, *they* can offer off-the-record comments, but all of your statements should be for the record. Assume that you are being evaluated the entire time you are on the firm's premises, even in the elevators and in the lobby. When you are sitting in the reception area waiting to be interviewed, there may be clients sitting beside you. Remember to behave in a professional manner at all times.

37. **Different Types of Interviews.** There are differences between a boutique law firm interview, a large law firm interview, a government interview, and a small city interview.

In a boutique law firm interview, you will almost invariably have to explain why you are interested in that particular boutique practice area. Whether it is labour, IP, or civil litigation, you must be able to answer the question. You will be competing against people who have known for years that they want to practise that particular type of law (e.g., labour law). The firm will be looking for people who are interested in exclusivity in their practice area. Be prepared for such questions.

In a large law firm interview, the interview might seem more casual because the interviewers may not require you to know the area in which you want to practise. If you work for a large law firm you will be rotating through practice areas. For this reason, the interviewers will be more interested in evaluating your trustworthiness and your ability to work with them as a colleague than in your preferred practice areas. They may ask for a general idea of the area in which you think you want to practise, but it is unlikely they will hold you to that statement. If you are interviewing for a summer rather than an articling job, some of the offices will ask you to pick a department where you would like to spend your entire summer. Be prepared to pick a department for the summer, but remain open to the rotation system for articling.

In a government interview, you will probably feel as if you are taking an oral exam. They will most likely ask you the pre-formatted questions that they ask every student. You may find the process impersonal. Some students find the government interview to be an easier type of interview because of its apparent transparency. It is likely that you will be asked questions about substantive areas of the law and about major pieces of legislation with which this particular government department works. They will probably score you on your responses. This method of evaluation means that if you answer a question and then a few minutes later you want to amplify your response, you can ask to add more to your earlier response. The interviewers may be able to go back into their notes and insert your amplified response.

In a small city interview, a long-term commitment to the small city may be more important than any specific skill or asset that is listed on your resumé. If you are applying to a small city or jurisdiction, you should expect questions about why you want to move to the jurisdiction and how long you plan to remain there, unless, of course, you are from that small city and plan to return to it. Smaller cities operate on local community principles and are not necessarily accustomed to the frequent job switching that occurs in larger markets. Whenever you apply to a law firm in a city that is not the city in which your law school is located, or is not the city in which you grew up, questions concerning your commitment to the city become relevant.

38. Interviewer Fatigue. Interviewer fatigue is a factor in the interview process as much as your own interview fatigue. If you see that your interviewer is getting tired, try to increase the energy level by speaking a bit louder, faster, or in a more animated manner. Remember, interviewer fatigue is about the interviewer; try not to take it personally. If you find yourself in this situation, it is up to you to generate energy for the duration of the interview. This situation is no different from one in which you are required to argue a motion at the end of the day and you can see that the judge is fatigued. A very tired interviewer will often revert to broad questions such as "tell me about yourself." These open-ended questions are easier to answer if you have prepared properly. You may find yourself in a better position to deliver lots of information when you are dealing with a fatigued interviewer.

39. Bad Interviews. If your interview is not going well, it may not be your fault. It may be the fault of a bad interviewer. If this is the case, then all of the interviews conducted by this particular lawyer did not go well. Try to take control of a bad interview in a subtle manner. Keep going and behave as if the interview is going well. If you find that the questions you are getting suggest that the interviewer is exhausted, offer the interviewer more information about yourself, even if the interviewer does not ask you to do so.

40. **Questions for Interviewers.** All career services offices have an excellent articles and books on behavioural interviewing techniques that include some sample questions for you to ask the interviewer. Behavioural interviewing (sometimes called strategic interviewing) is an interviewing style opted for by many of the large law firms. It is based on the premise that your past behaviour is a good indicator of your future behaviour and performance. Always prepare a good questions for your interviewers. The questions you ask will reveal your level of interest in the firm, the research you have done, and what is important to you. Do not ask questions for which the answers are readily available on the law firm's website; however, feel free to ask the firm to elaborate on information found on their website.

41. **Elaborate on Your Resumé.** Be prepared to explain aspects of your resumé in detail. If an interviewer observes that you were a swim instructor when you were twelve years old do not simply reply, "Yes, I was." You should say, "Yes, and in fact, I was the youngest swim instructor they ever hired and it was my first real leadership experience." Follow this response with a thirty-second explanation of how you developed as a person as a result of this experience. All interview questions, and this goes back to the motivation behind the questions in an interview, are designed to enable the firm to understand you better. You should view an interviewer's questions as opportunities to offer more information about yourself and to articulate how you are developing as a professional.

42. **Repeated Questions.** Some students find that they are asked the same questions in each of their interviews during a single recruitment cycle. In fact, sometimes these questions are repeated through consecutive recruitment cycles (e.g., in summer and articling position interviews). This might be because there is something very interesting on your resumé, or that you have done something unique. If you find that you are being asked the same question, then prepare a really good response during a break between interviews. Improve your answer every time you get asked the same question. Never embarrass an interviewer by pointing out that you have been asked this question ten times before.

43. **Repeated Answers.** Be prepared to be asked the same question by different interviewers, especially within the same law firm. Repeated questions are especially common during a large law firm interview in which you are shuttled from one office to another to meet different interviewers who may not have time to speak with each other before interviewing you. If this happens, you have to learn to hit the repeat button in your brain and answer the question as if it has never been asked of you before. You are being evaluated on each interview and not on your overall performance in the set of interviews as a whole. To add a bit of variation, refer back to your prior answer and say, "I gave a lengthier explanation to Sandra when I was interviewing with her earlier, but I can summarize my paper as follows . . . ." This advice is useful when you know that the interviewer is really just drop-

ping by the interview for about five minutes, and the original interviewer is still in the room. Be prepared to match the level of formality of the person interviewing you. You may find that you need to vary your style, even within one firm's set of interviews. Do not get frustrated by the repetition. If you inadvertently communicate a sense of frustration, for example, in your facial expression, the interviewers might misinterpret the situation and assume that you are irritated by them.

44. **Firm Tours.** Ask if you can go on a firm tour. Ask to see the library; this is where you are going to be spending most of your time as a summer and articling student. The firm tour is also a great opportunity to observe the differences between firms. Some offices have excellent in-house libraries while other law firms' libraries are not very good. Law firms with smaller libraries may send you to the court house library or to a law school library, if there is one near their offices.

    Also, take note of who is in the library. Are there only students in the library or do you see senior partners? It is a good sign if the senior lawyers are doing research in the library. Be sure to shake the hand of the librarian. The librarian will be a very important person in your life, whether you are a summer or an articling student.

45. **Firm Evaluation.** Remember, you are evaluating the firms using the same criteria that they are using to evaluate you. You are entering into a business relationship. Can you trust them? Do you want to work with them? Do they share your values? Are they going to allow you to do other things that are important to you during your summer or articling experience? Evaluate them and judge them. If they are encouraging you to deviate from the recruitment rules, judge them accordingly. Rules are exceptionally important to lawyers. Honesty and integrity are the gatekeepers of these rules. You should take all rules very seriously. If you find that a firm is playing around with the rules, you can reasonably make conclusions about how they work with their clients.

46. **Hidden Interviews.** Cocktail parties and dinners can be *hidden* interviews. These events appear to be setting you up for a social experience; however, the interviewers are evaluating you on the same criteria as they would during a formal interview. Remember, this is still an interview, only now the interviewers are evaluating you in a social environment. Pay attention during the cocktail parties to the fact that you are still being interviewed. The cocktail party is not the time for off-the-record conversations or a time to test your alcohol endurance. It is also not the time to order three desserts and taste test each of them.

47. **Attending a Dinner.** Arrange practice dinners. Each year, students get together with their friends and practise eating together as though they were attending an interview dinner. They go to a cheap restaurant and practise answering questions while eating. They also try to determine what types of food are easy to eat and what types are potentially embarrassing. Surprisingly, salads can be difficult to eat during a conversation. Food that can be cut into bite-sized portions is easier to manage dur-

ing a business lunch or dinner. Drippy foods and finger foods can be the cause of embarrassment.

48. **Drinking at Dinners.** Limit yourself to one drink at dinner. Counter-balance the alcohol with some caffeine if you find that the alcohol relaxes you too much. Try to resist any pressure placed upon you to match the lawyers' alcohol consumption at all of these functions, especially at casual parties hosted at pubs or bars. Remember, you are going to dinner with lawyers who may be ten to twenty years your senior and they probably have been drinking socially for many more years than you.

49. **Thank-you Letters.** You do not need to send a thank-you note after an on-campus interview because it is not a formal interview, but rather a pre-screening interview. However, you may wish to send thank-you notes after a full interview with a firm at its office. If you choose to do so, send a single e-mail or letter to the firm recruiter (the person to whom you addressed your application). The firm recruiter will have a copy of your interview schedule with the firm and will forward the e-mail to the lawyers with whom you met. The firms are bombarded with student e-mails during peak recruiting times and have little time to respond. If you send a thank-you note, you should keep it brief: two to three sentences will suffice.

50. **Follow-up E-mails.** Most students overuse e-mail. Lawyers are reluctant to put their personal opinions or comments in writing. When conducting any sort of follow-up after an interview (to find out about waitlists or to find out why you did not get hired), you should consider placing a telephone call. You may find the prospect of a follow-up telephone call daunting, but it is the best method for getting feedback. An e-mail follow-up is too impersonal. If you send an e-mail, the lawyers do not know if you are angry, upset, or frustrated. They cannot deduce your tone from an e-mail and the tone of your question will affect how they respond to your questions. A telephone call allows for the personal touch that is needed when asking these questions.

Professionalism in Interviews

When preparing for an interview, it may be helpful to approach it from a larger philosophical perspective. Consider where you are on the larger map outlining the stages in your life between law school and your career as a lawyer. At this point in time, you are shedding your student persona and you are beginning to develop into a professional lawyer.

There are three complaints that students regularly make when confronted with an interview process:

1. This process seems artificial. I don't want to go to all the cocktail parties.
2. I don't like the game that goes along with the interview process.
3. I am who I am. I don't want to change who I am for the firms.

In order to overcome the issues raised in these complaints, it is important that you understand the rationale that underlies the interview process and that you remain focused on your immediate goal, which is to get a job. At the same time, it is very important for you to ensure that you do not compromise your values when you are seeking a job. If you find that there is an aspect of the recruitment process that is so unpleasant that it contradicts your values, you should consider applying for jobs in another manner. Speak with your career services office about the many different ways you can enter the job market and the different recruitment programs that each city offers.

1. **This Process Seems Artificial.** The interview process is not designed to be pleasant. Formal recruitment processes that see hundreds of students apply and get hired within a matter of weeks are designed primarily to be efficient, to be fair to students, and to level the playing field for law firms. Do not become upset with yourself or with the process if you are not particularly enjoying what you have to go through to get a job. Many students do not like writing exams, but what is important about the exam process is the end product: a law degree. At the end of interviewing, you will get a job (eventually, at least). The fact that the process is unpleasant does not take away from the fact that it is worthwhile.

2. **It's All a Game.** Planning your future career is *not* a game. Try to turn the concept around on its head. The interviewing process is not a game, but it may involve game-like strategies. What you do when you play a game requires deliberate steps, strategic decisions, and ability (usually the result of lots of practise). This is true of sports, board games, cards, video games, etc. It is important to be able to draw from all the strategies and techniques that you developed over the years when you were learning to play new games. The interview process requires deliberate and strategic moves on your part. The more conscious you are of the strategy involved, the better you will be at it.

3. **I Am Who I Am.** You are not being asked to change as a person. When recruiters speak about dressing conservatively for an interview, they are talking about the fact that you are not going to be a student forever, nor are you going to dress like a student forever. You are about to move into the professional world and accept new responsibilities, the seriousness of which you may have never experienced before.

   Everyone who begins a new career enters into a system of change, both private and public. This system of change should be embraced, not resisted. Pay attention to these changes now, when you are in the process of applying for jobs, rather than waiting until after you start a job. These changes do not mean that there is going to be a fundamental change in who you are. They will probably be part of a progressive process, given the new professional context that you will be entering.

Law firms interview you to discover your ability, personality, and attitude in a business and professional setting. These characteristics, viewed collectively, are sometimes thought to define an individual's work ethic. All of your preparation for an interview, including the content of what you will say as well as how you present yourself, should be focused on the goal of presenting a professional work ethic.

Physiology and the Interview

Physical Reactions

Remember, you are already an expert in the type of experience that you will be embarking on in an interview, even if you have never gone through a professional interview before. Your expertise comes from your exam-writing experience.

Everyone goes through a different range of experiences before and while writing an exam, but most get a rush of adrenaline in the first few minutes of an exam. It is the same for an interview and it will be the same when you go to court to argue a case. Adrenaline is a burst of energy that you should try to control and utilize productively. Breathing helps, as does drinking water, as both slow down your mind and body. You may find that your ears ring, your mouth gets dry, or your hands get clammy. Each person's physical response is different from that of others. Just work through it and keep going. In most cases, experience makes these chemical responses much more tolerable.

Most importantly, do not jump to the conclusion that the interview is going badly. Most interviewers expect students to be somewhat nervous and they will be tolerant if you get off to a shaky start. In many cases, what you are experiencing will not be observed by the interviewer. Your nervousness will probably go unnoticed, unless you comment on it. Keep going and focus on the content of the interview.

The most common effect of interview nervousness is perspiration. This is natural and something we really cannot do anything about, despite the claims of many antiperspirant companies. Rather than trying to find a way to stop sweating, think about what you can wear to mask the effect so that you do not need to be self-conscious. For instance, if you are wearing a suit, you may want to keep your jacket on, even if others in the room remove theirs. For longer interview days, consider bringing an extra shirt or blouse in your briefcase to change into at midday if necessary. If you tend to clench your hands when nervous, try to remember to keep your hands (especially your right hand) open and relaxed during your interview. It is likely that you will shake the interviewer's hand at the end of the interview.

If your mouth becomes dry, keep away from gum because there is a risk that you might forget to discard it before the interview (it is very bad form to interview while chewing gum). To avoid developing a dry mouth, ask for water at the beginning of the interview and carry some mints.

If you get a headache from nervousness, avoid caffeine and alcohol, both of which can dehydrate you and make your headache worse. Drink lots of water and be sure to bring tablets of your preferred analgesic. If you forget, most office towers have convenience stores at the ground level where you can purchase headache medication. Also, consider bringing a snack bar or a power bar for a burst of energy between interviews.

Calm Down the Night Before

The night before an interview, do something that is relaxing, distracting, and enjoyable. In the days leading up to an interview, try to slowly change your attitude towards interview. Do not think of yourself as a student interviewing for a job, but rather as a colleague meeting with another colleague. Keep in mind that firms indicate repeatedly that they are attempting to determine whether they can be colleagues with each job candidate. Remember, once you get called to the Bar, your interviewers will become your professional colleagues.

After the Interview

In the same way that you slow down after an exam, you may find yourself becoming tired after interviewing, especially if you have more than two interviews in one day. This exhaustion can become a problem when you are taking part in formal recruitment processes because, following your interviews, you may be required to make very important decisions within a very short period of time.

There are a couple of things you can do to help maintain energy level and stay alert after interviews. First, be sure to take notes immediately after an interview while your energy level is relatively high and before your body has slowed down. These notes will be important to you later on when you are tired, but you still have decisions to make. It is very important to make a decision about what job to accept based on relevant factors, not on minor afterthoughts that remain in your mind simply because you are tired.

After your interviews, consider going for a walk, getting some fresh air, or doing a light workout to release the tension that builds up during the interviews. These activities may generate a second energy spurt that will help you to make clear decisions after the interviews are over.

If you are invited to receptions or dinners after a day of interviewing, it is important to maintain your energy level throughout the evening. Consider the difference between runners who sprint one hundred metres and those who run marathons. If you know that your endurance will be tested through the interview process, be sure to conserve as much energy as possible early on. For longer days of interviews, it is important to eat nutritious food frequently throughout the day and remain hydrated in order to avoid a headache. Also, if possible, try to go for a walk between interviews to get some fresh air and re-energize.

Dialogic Theory

We all know that language mediates experience and our perception of reality. Prior to your interview, the interviewer only has information about you that you provided in your cover letter, resumé, transcripts and anything else that went into your application package. She knows nothing else about you. When you walk into an interview, the interviewer has about an hour (for OCIs, only twenty minutes) to gain a tremendous amount of information about you, all of which will come from the words that you speak and from non-linguistic language. Non-linguistic language includes information that comes from physical gestures, facial expressions and from your general disposition.

When you are in a dynamic communication system, such as an interview, both speakers are motivated to try to incorporate the other person into their sphere in order to create a positive dialogue.

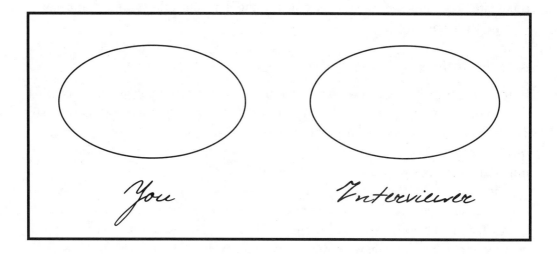

Your goal, throughout your interview, is to extend as much of your sphere into the interviewer's sphere as possible. At the same time, the interviewer, through her questions, will be trying to extend her sphere into your sphere. These concurrent processes produce a space where the two spheres overlap. It is within this space that you and the interviewer will find a *shared reality*.

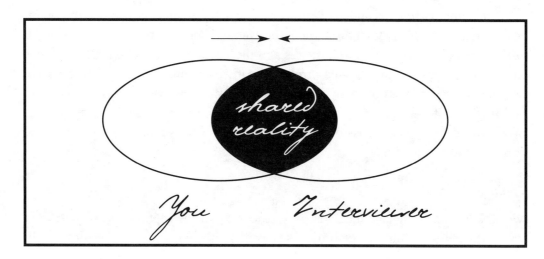

Ideally, the overlapping space should be as large as possible. The space represents your shared experience. When you answer questions during an interview, try to speak to the middle area where the spheres overlap. The more you can make the space grow by communicating experiences that the interviewer shares, the more likely it is that the interviewer is going to think of you as a colleague.

What does this mean in practical terms? Consider the student who is concerned that he will not be able to explain to his interviewer that he did not have a summer job without sounding as though he could not get hired. There are several responses he could make to an interviewer who asks, "What did you do this summer?" What is important is that he is truthful and that he attempts to speak to what is likely a shared experience. If the student responds, "I tried to get a job, but I could not find one," the student risks moving away from the middle, shared experience because the interviewer is an employed person and may never have been unemployed. On the other hand the student could respond, "It was my last summer off before becoming a lawyer so I spent the summer playing baseball with my nephew in the park," or "I traveled using the money I saved from working part-time during law school." Suddenly, the student has gone straight to the middle of the two spheres and reminded the interviewer of his or her last summer as a student. Also, by mentioning a nephew or traveling, the student may have moved into another shared experience (the interviewer may be a parent or may have traveled as well).

three: **First Year**

Recruitment Cycles for First-Year Law Students

When you look at your law school's website and when you visit the career services office (or articling office, depending on the law school you attend), you may find an overwhelming amount of information about career opportunities. This is especially the case when you visit the job-posting boards, whether they are on a website or in a binder.

As a first-year student, it is sometimes helpful to assume that you are interested in everything. There is no reason to rule anything out, unless you know exactly why you came to law school and you are seeking out a specific education. At the beginning of your law education, you can choose from a large number of potential career opportunities. At this stage in your career, you should not place restrictions on yourself. Most first-year students do not have a defined career plan; many have not even made up their minds as to whether they intend to practise law or do something else with their law degrees. In part, the first-year academic curriculum is designed to provide you with a broad overview of the various areas of law for this very reason. Throughout the year, the career services office at your law school will likely run seminars on different practice areas and career options for those with law degrees. From these seminars, you will learn what is available well before you have to make any real decisions about your career plans.

Keep in mind that if you do get a job in one area of law for a summer, there is no reason to rule out moving into another area of practice or into another career altogether at a later date. The ability to shift areas of interest is sometimes referred to as professional mobility. In other words, if you get a summer job at a criminal office, you do not have to be a criminal lawyer forever. As obvious as this sounds, students frequently express concern about becoming pigeon-holed. Your ability to be mobile throughout the various recruitment systems will depend on your ability to research and analyze your opportunities effectively and to express your written and oral advocacy skills in your cover letter and interview. What you learn in a criminal office, for instance, has collateral value in many other practice areas. The experience of working in any law office — seeing how files are managed, meeting with clients, understanding how legal research is conducted and applied to a file, going to court, and watching how lawyers spend their day — is valuable no matter what area of practice you end up pursuing.

Fall Term: First Year

First-year recruitment continues to be rare in the Canadian law market. Many first-year students find that they return to the summer job that they had before they entered law school. As frustrating as this may sound at first, there are reasons for it. For example, the law you learn in first year is very general and difficult to apply to client cases. The situation changes when you enter into your upper-year courses.

First-year students are usually surprised to learn that there are few job postings for them in the fall term of first year and some career services offices even refuse to see first-year students until after their first term is substantially finished. Almost all US and Canadian law schools belong to NALP (National Association of Law Placement), an organization that maintains guidelines on, among other things, the recruitment of first-year students. These guidelines operate on the principle that it is important to get first-year law students settled into their classes and focused on their academic studies before the students are encouraged to start thinking about recruitment and career development.

In fact, some jurisdictions, such as the City of Toronto, are specifically prohibited by their province's law society from recruiting first-year students before January (i.e., the beginning of the second term of first year). Again, this rule is based on the principle that first-year students should be given time to focus on their academic programs before they look for jobs.

Your career services office will provide you with ample notice of the deadlines and procedures for the very few first-year recruitment programs for first-year summer jobs that do exist in the fall term. There are recruitment programs for jobs in Ottawa (law firms with intellectual property practices only), Calgary, and the Atlantic Provinces among other cities. Vancouver is a much less-regulated jurisdiction, despite its size, so there are a few law firms that may entertain first-year student applications for summer jobs in the fall term. If you have an interest in any of these cities, it might be worthwhile to visit your career services office, once you have settled into your classes and bought your books, so that you can become informed about all the relevant deadlines.

Also, if you are from a smaller city or a city that does not have any formal summer student recruitment rules, or if you plan on working in a remote jurisdiction, law firms in these areas may be interested in hearing from you during your first year (probably during your second term). These areas include cities and jurisdictions such as the territories (Yukon, Northwest Territories, and Nunavut), Prince George, Red Deer, Moose Jaw, North Bay, Niagara Falls, Peterborough, Cape Breton, etc.

Information Sessions

During the fall term, many law schools will run information sessions or seminars to introduce students to the variety of law practices and areas of law that are available. Frequently, the law schools will invite lawyers and alumni to speak about their law practices and how they developed their careers. These programs are useful for several reasons. First, you can learn about new and emerging areas of law or areas that are not commonly discussed. For instance, students who are interested in health law may find it useful to learn that you can practise health law in the form of mental incompetency and guardianship litigation, medical malpractice, and capacity board hearings. These are all different sub-specialties under the same practice heading of health law. Also, corporate law has different sub-specialties such as securities law, commercial law, and corporate restructuring and can be practised at a law firm, as in-house counsel to a company, and within the government in their various business and finance branches.

Second, the more you learn about these sub-categories and different areas of law, the more you will expand your understanding of the value of your law degree and be able to explore with confidence your specific interests. Sometimes these seminars trigger a particular interest in students that they might not otherwise have discovered. Remember that some of these sub-specialties take years to learn. You may find that you begin your career in a general area of practice and then proceed to increase your understanding of a specialty area as you gain more experience with certain files. Also, these seminars will increase your knowledge and enable you to speak more intelligently and comprehensively about your understanding of different areas of law during an interview.

Perhaps the most valuable aspect of these seminars is the opportunity to meet lawyers who practise law every day. These days, many law students enter law school without previously having met anyone who is a lawyer. As a result, their concept what it is to be a lawyer comes from the media and the entertainment industry. The opportunity to speak to lawyers and ask questions about how they integrate their practice with their own lives, how they developed their practice, and why they like their area of law, has much more value than reading a law firm's brochure or website. Also, the lawyers who come to speak to law students usually offer very wise tips to students on how to survive interviews and articling.

Career Fairs

If you find out that your law school runs a career fair, attend it as early in your education as possible. Career fairs are very useful. Many students attend the career fairs every year until they get an articling job. Career fairs are usually large programs that are often held off campus in a hotel ballroom or in a nearby convention centre. At most career fairs, law offices set up tables, either alphabetically or by city. Students move through the room, picking up brochures and speaking with the representatives of the law offices. Career fairs are very good opportunities to gain a lot of general information about job opportunities. They also afford you the opportunity to speak to a few representatives about their law offices. In fact, career fairs have proven to be so helpful to students that some law schools now hold several fairs, including government career fairs, public interest career fairs, and traditional law firm fairs.

If your law school circulates a booklet of the names of the law offices that will be attending your career fair, try to read through the booklet the night before so that you can target firms that interest you and build a strategy before you enter the career fair. Because there are sometimes 200–400 people in a career fair at one time, the situation can become overwhelming and you may feel quite anonymous. Try to resist the temptation to zip through the room with your best friend and grab brochures without introducing yourself. There is more than enough time for you to have substantial conversations with a half a dozen to a dozen lawyers at the fair. Also, consider visiting the table that doesn't have a long line up of students. The lawyer at the quieter table will probably be better able to have a substantial conversation with you because he will not be distracted by hoards of students.

Many law students become quite shy when speaking with lawyers. Here are a few questions you can ask lawyers at a career fair:

1. What area of law do you practise?
2. How did you get into this area of law?
3. How long have you been with this law office?
4. Why do you enjoy working at this law office and in this area of law?
5. What courses and extra-curricular activities would you recommend I take if I am interested in this area of law?

A conversation stemming from these questions will likely take from five to eight minutes.

Remember to introduce yourself and take the lawyers' business cards (or write down their names). If you have a good, lengthy conversation with a representative at a career fair, you may want to reference the conversation in a cover letter if you apply to the law office at a later date. If so, it is important that you remember the name of the person with whom you spoke at the career fair.

Law school career fairs are generally not the time to circulate your resumé, even if you are accustomed to doing so at other industry career fairs. In fact, unless your law school advises you otherwise, handing out your resumé during a career fair may be considered poor form. Instead, speak with the representatives at the fair, take their business cards, and forward your resumé to them after the event if invited to do so and in accordance with what the representative tells you is their recruitment timing.

Because there are so few first-year summer jobs, a first-year student may be attending the career fair for information purposes and general introductions rather than for a specific job search. You would be surprised at how well lawyers remember meeting students. When you attend the same career fair the following year, as a second-year student, you may find that a representative remembers you and the conversation he had with you the previous year. If this is the case, take the opportunity to build on your earlier conversation with him.

Get Involved in Law School

At every first-year fall orientation program in every law school across Canada, upper-year students speak about the value of getting involved in your law school either through the student government, legal aid programs, moots, law journals or newspapers, as research assistants for professors, or through other social programs. From the perspective of developing a career plan, this is a very wise idea for at least two reasons. First, becoming involved, especially in legal aid programs, gives you the opportunity to work with clients, and on files, and to learn about different areas of law. Second, law firms typically seek out active law students so becoming actively involved in your law school will help you at the application stage and give you something substantial to talk about during an interview.

When lawyers look back on their law school days, even twenty or thirty years after they graduate, they often remember their extra-curricular involvement more than what they learned in their torts or contracts classes. This is another reason to consider getting involved.

For those students who are concerned that studying, parenting, or maintaining a part-time job will consume all their time, remember the adage "if you need to get something done, give it to a busy person." If you spend even three hours once a week on a pro bono file or on a law school committee, the collateral learning that occurs from this extra-curricular work will likely make you more efficient in your study methods.

December-Break Preparation

Most first-year students are understandably exhausted after their first-term exams in December and want to do nothing more than rest during the break. Resting up for the second term is wise, but it is also advisable to spend a couple of days on some preparatory job application work before you return to law school. January is as busy a time as

September, and many first-year students are surprised at the increased pace of their classes in the winter term.

If your law school prepares a career guide or another resource guide, consider reading it over the holidays. If you have not done so yet, visit your law school's career services website so that you have a sense of its comprehensiveness and bookmark pages that are of particular interest to you. Also, have a shot at drafting a resumé and a cover letter. The first time you do it, it will take you much longer than you expect. Some students spend a full day playing around with tabs and margins before they get the hang of resumé writing. Others find it difficult to get beyond writing the first sentence of a cover letter. These frustrating starts are normal, especially if you have never drafted a professional resumé or cover letter before. However, once you have a good draft of a resumé and cover letter ready for use, applying for a job can be accomplished with relative ease.

Winter Term: First Year

January is the deadline for first-year summer job applications for a small group of Bay Street firms in Toronto that hire first-year students. These interviews take place in mid-February, during or near reading week, depending on which law school you attend. This is one of the most competitive recruitment programs in Canada, in part because so few firms participate in first-year recruitment and because there are so few positions available. It is far more competitive than the second-year recruitment program for these same firms that is conducted through on-campus interviews (OCIs). In some years, there are as few as thirty-five positions available for first-year summer students in the major Bay Street law firms, compared with over three hundred and fifty summer positions available to second-year students. Most students who apply for first-year summer jobs at these firms do not get interviews, so you should not be discouraged from reapplying in second year.

Most summer job postings for law students across Canada are posted in the winter term from February to May. Each law school will have a different method of disseminating this information, but most either send broadcast e-mails to the student body or post the jobs on a password-protected page on their websites. Be sure to understand how your law school notifies its students of jobs and ensure that you are current with this method of communication. Almost every law school will offer a computer terminal, either in their law library or student services area, for those students who do not have access to the internet or e-mail from home. If you are having difficulty receiving job-posting information, speak to your career services office and they may be able to accommodate you in another way or partner you with a student on your articling committee who does have this access.

When reading job postings as a first-year student, it is important to differentiate job postings for articling positions and those for summer positions. Unless you are applying to an office in the Atlantic provinces (Nova Scotia, New Brunswick, PEI, and Newfoundland), you can not apply for an articling position when you are in first year. Also, if you are in a four-year law program joint with another degree, many law firms and recruitment programs will consider you to be a first-year student twice (i.e., in your first year in the law program and then in your first year in the other program). Only a select few firms will accept applications from students who are in their first year of a four year program. Be sure to check if you qualify for first-year jobs if you are in the first year of a four-year program before you apply.

Once you have isolated the summer job postings, be sure to apply only to those that indicate that they will consider first-year students. If you observe that a summer job posting for a second-year student is still available several weeks beyond its deadline date, it may be an indication that the office was unsuccessful in finding a suitable second-year candidate. In such a case, you can speak with your career services office about whether it would be advisable for you to apply for the job. If you have a specific background that matches the job posting (for instance, if the job is at a law firm specializing in tax and you have an accounting degree or practised as an accountant before you came to law school), you may be a competitive candidate for the position, despite the fact that you are a first-year student.

One of the biggest employers of first-year summer law students are the law schools themselves. There are often a number of research assistantships available as well as opportunities to work in administrative positions. In addition, the various legal aid offices, law journals, and other ancillary faculty programs (e.g., innocence projects, constitutional law programs, women's studies centres, mediation centres, and Aboriginal centres) also hire summer students. These are excellent opportunities to focus on an area of law, gain legal work experience, and remain involved with your law school during the summer.

In addition to your law school summer job options, be sure to review all the employment opportunities within the larger university environment that are not necessarily posted at the law school. You may be required to obtain a password or login code for the central career centre at your university because few law schools duplicate these job postings on their law school websites. Law students are traditionally very competitive candidates for these positions because of their ability to process large volumes of information quickly, their diligence, their high standards of performance, and their strong work ethic. Be sure to highlight these aspects of your portfolio when applying for general university positions.

How to Approach Recruitment Cycles

Everyone loves statistics, especially law students. It is important to remember that statistics only provide indications about group behaviour. When you read through the statistics produced by your law school, remember that the information does not predict your individual likelihood of success, but rather provides a summary of past group results.

Getting a job is difficult, no matter what industry you are in. It sometimes takes as much time and as much work as studying for a whole course. All too often, students do not leave enough time to apply properly for jobs and then find that they can not accomplish their goals. Be sure to give yourself the time that you need to get yourself a job. This is another reason why taking a shot at a cover letter and resumé during the December break is a good idea.

The formal recruitment programs are designed to make things easier for students. They are designed to promote efficiency and fairness, but there are inevitably downsides to operating in this manner. One downside is that it compresses everyone together into a group and this increases the stress on the individual student and on the group as a whole. Group stress can be unproductive and can have a negative effect on an individual student and his ability to think independently throughout the process. When taking part in interviews during a group recruitment program, you will still need to prepare for the interview privately and reflect on your personal values in order to evaluate whether the job is suitable for you.

Remember that the first year of your law program is primarily designed to introduce you to legal concepts (from an academic point of view) and to legal career options (from a professional perspective). There is no expectation in the profession that you will commit yourself to one area of study in your first year of law school. In addition, there is no expectation that you will seek out a law-related first-year summer job. You will have plenty of time in your second and third years of law school to concentrate on a particular area of law.

Legal Research and Writing

Legal research and writing is one of the most important courses you will take in law school (note that the course title will vary, depending on your law school). The course will have value while you are in law school, during your career search, and once you are called to the Bar.

More than ever before, the law firms across Canada, especially the smaller offices and boutique practices, are beginning to ask for writing samples from students for articling and even for summer job applications. Effective written advocacy is essential to a successful lawyer and the firms have realized that requiring students to establish their ability to write well from the outset is an important way for them to differentiate between candidates.

Many students, especially those who come from science or accounting undergraduate programs, do not have solid writing samples ready to submit with a job application. As a result, the writing that they do in their legal research and writing course may become a writing sample for a job application. If this is the case, it is very important to pay attention to the class and practise your writing skills as frequently as possible. To this end, students without significant writing backgrounds should consider writing the occasional article for their student newspaper.

As with anything that you do, whether it is learning how to drive a car or how to play tennis, the first time you try it you are likely to perform relatively poorly compared with how you will perform after you have practised considerably. The same goes for your written and oral advocacy training. You need to write frequently in order to excel at it.

Your ability to research effectively is also essential to your success as a lawyer and will have an impact on the success of your clients. There is a matrix in legal research that can be best articulated in a triangle. As a law student, and once you are a lawyer, you will be interacting with all three aspects of this matrix at all times.

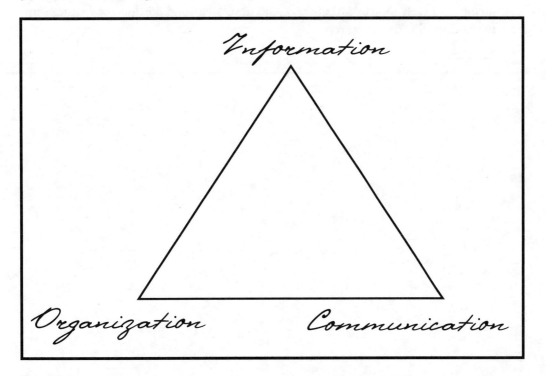

Information

Legal research is now much more accessible to everyone, even to the public. Gone are the days when a large law firm in a big city was considered better because its library was more comprehensive than a small firm in a regional office. As a result of on-line research enterprises, such as LexisNexis's Quicklaw and Carswell's Westlaw, there is now equivalency among offices and cities as far as access to the law goes. In fact, over the past ten years we have witnessed an almost complete democratization of access to case law.

Organization and Communication

Given the equivalency of access to the law, the problem that new lawyers now face is the fact that there seems to be too much information and not enough time to digest it all. In an environment where legal research is accessible to everyone, those who can organize and communicate information efficiently will be best able to achieve their clients' goals. Law school provides training in all three areas: understanding core information (academic classes), organizing information efficiently (exam summaries), and communicating information effectively (exams, essays, and memos).

Documentary work will dominate your experience as a lawyer. Memo writing, motion drafting, factum writing, legal opinions, legislation recommendations, and summaries of transcripts are all examples of the types of documentary work that you will be doing constantly in a law practice. Devote time to developing these skills now, pay attention in class, practise frequently, and develop a solid portfolio of writing samples to use during your job search.

four : **Second Year**

Second-Year Summer Jobs

Although most law schools offer extensive seminars on how to find an articling job, they offer comparatively few seminars on how to find a suitable second-year summer job. Second-year law students may find this frustrating, particularly those who did not pursue first-year summer jobs that were career related.

Because it is now customary for law students to have law office and file experience by the time they apply for articling positions, many students seek out a second-year summer job with a law firm. Students who do not find summer jobs in law offices can still gain valuable experience that will help them to further their law careers. When you are looking for a second-year summer job, it is important to consider your articling goals. Choose a second-year summer job that will allow you to fill in the gaps on your resumé, a job that will make you a more competitive candidate when you apply for articling positions in the future. It is also time to start considering in which city you wish to article. It is a good idea to begin to establish roots in that city through a summer job.

If you wish to conduct preparatory research on summer positions, read through the job postings for the previous year so that you can see what opportunities were available and when those opportunities arose. Take note of the employers that interest you and the practice areas that you find intriguing. Consider whether these opportunities will help you to further your career plans and begin to build a bridge so that you can achieve your articling goals.

Most law schools have extensive summer job-posting lists that are either web-based or available on job-posting boards. As a first-year student, you may have viewed these postings with frustration because they were only open to second-year students. These postings are typically from law firms, in-house counsel law departments in corporations, government law offices, various law school departments, non-profit legal organizations, and other law-related industries (e.g., insurance companies, banks).

If you already know with which firm you would like to article, it is worthwhile to see if the office hires summer students. If you do not know where you want to article, but you know the general area that you want to article in, seek out job postings in that general area. For example, if you have an interest in family law, look for job postings with firms that offer family law or offices where family law issues arise (e.g., children's aid society). Many students remain with their summer employer for their articling. There has been a growing trend in law firms and government offices to increase summer job opportunities so that they can attract articling students through their summer programs. This is good news for second-year law students who are eager to attain practical law office experience.

Most law offices in larger Canadian cities have an agreement with other law firms in their cities with respect to application deadlines for summer program positions. In most cases, an agreement specifies the *earliest* date that a law office can set for an application deadline. The agreement allows law offices within a given city to set application deadlines later than the deadline stated in the agreement, if they wish. For instance, Toronto and Vancouver each have very early second-year summer application deadlines: in September of second year. Many smaller offices in these cities are not prepared to begin recruiting summer students as early as September. September deadlines are useful for larger law offices that recruit across the country and can commit to hiring students ten months in advance of a summer start date, but the early deadline is not as useful for smaller offices. Smaller offices often wish to commit to hiring a single summer student in March or April for a job that may begin in May. Also, some offices (both large and small) will not hire second-year summer students until the students have fall-term transcripts available to submit with their applications.

Many students begin to prepare their application material for early fall-term recruitment programs in August so that they are not overwhelmed with extra work when school begins in September. Toronto has the most formalized early fall-term recruitment program. In Toronto, summer candidates are processed through a preliminary screening system known as on-campus interviews (OCIs).[1] Toronto is the most popular

---

1   Refer to the section entitled "On-Campus Interviews (OCIs) for Positions with Law Firms in Toronto" on pages 42–48 for a detailed explanation of how OCIs operate.

destination for summer and articling students in Canada. The large law firms in Toronto receive up to seven hundred applications per recruitment cycle every year.

The next most popular destinations for summer positions are Vancouver, Ottawa, and Calgary. Vancouver's summer application deadlines are typically set at the end of September. In Ottawa, law firms with intellectual property practices set October deadlines for summer applications. Most Ottawa law firms recruit summer students during the winter term, usually in February. In Calgary, some firms set their deadlines for summer applications in October, but other firms set November and even December deadlines.

Law firms in the Atlantic Provinces begin to recruit summer students in the fall term of second year. In the Atlantic Provinces, students do not apply for summer positions; they apply and interview for articling positions only. If a student obtains an articling job, the student is also hired on as a summer student. This process is very different from summer recruitment programs elsewhere in Canada. In the rest of Canada, there is no guarantee that a summer position will automatically lead to an articling position. That said, most students who summer in a law office remain with their summer employer for articling.

Summer law firm jobs should not be looked upon as an opportunity to *city hop*. If you apply for a position in a province that is not the province of your law school, or, if you apply for a position in a province other than the province in which you grew up, you may find that you are questioned as to whether you intend to live permanently in the city in which the law firm is situated.[2]

Applying and interviewing for summer jobs is very good preparation for articling applications and interviews. Most law offices conduct their summer job interviews in the same way that they conduct their articling interviews. In addition, offices often use the same lawyers to conduct both summer and articling interviews. As a result, a firm's interviewing style tends to remain constant: either casual, semi-formal, or formal. All of the advice given in this book on applying and interviewing for articling positions (job applications, interviews, and research) also applies to summer applications. Remember that any in application process — whether it is for summer or articling positions — you are entering into the professional arena and interacting with your future colleagues. It is wise to treat your summer applications as seriously as your articling applications.

The main difference between summer and articling recruitment is that law offices do not expect you to have the same understanding of your practice preferences when you interview for summer positions as they do when you interview for articling positions. The law firms, especially those that conduct interviews for summer positions during the fall term of second year, will understand that your knowledge of the law is still quite general. When you interview for a summer position, do not hesitate to speak freely about areas of practice that you find interesting, but with which you have rela-

---

2   Refer to the section entitled "Articling in Another Province" on pages 59–60 for advice on out-of-province applications.

tively little experience. When you indicate an area of interest during your articling interviews, the firms will have the expectation that you have either taken a course in the area or that you know you will be studying the topic in your third year. Articling interviews occur in the spring and summer after second-year exams; therefore, it is likely that you will have already selected your third-year courses.

Most large, national, full-service firms will place you in one or two departments for the entire summer. For this reason, you will need to communicate a preference for certain practice areas when you apply to large, full-service firms, either in your cover letter or certainly by the time you interview with a firm. Communicating a preference does not lock you into an area forever. You can simply describe your developing areas of interest in your cover letter and then point out the area you are leaning towards and why. For instance, "I entered law school with the intention of working in corporate law, but I have recently developed a keen interest in energy law issues." This type of sentence does not oblige you to practise a single area of law, but it clearly expresses your emerging preferences.

If you apply to a boutique firm that practises in one area of law exclusively, it is very important for you to match your area of interest precisely with their practice area in order to be a competitive candidate. Boutique firms are well known for how focused their lawyers are in one area of law; the firms want to find students who are similarly focused during summer recruitment. For example, if you apply to a law firm that deals with intellectual property exclusively, it is your responsibility to be clear that intellectual property is your sole focus and to have a reasonable explanation as to why you want to practise this type of law. Typically, students develop this type of focus either through their undergraduate studies or through their work experience (before they arrived at law school). In such cases, it is wise to write a couple of sentences, or even a paragraph, in your cover letter explaining your endeavours before law school.

Increasingly, government offices are granting interviews to second-year summer students. Your law school will tell you in advance if this is the case. When applying to government offices, it is a good idea to design an entirely different cover letter from the one you design for private law firms. Government offices seek out students who are committed to servicing the public and working in the public interest; therefore, it is important to communicate your commitment in your cover letter. A government office is likely to question you on your understanding of the work that is performed in its department and the legislation that they most often use. All of this research can be conducted by reviewing websites and by reading the relevant statutes.

On-Campus Interviews (OCIs) for Positions with Law Firms in Toronto

The recruitment process known as on-campus interviews (OCIs) is foreign to many law students and is used in only a few other industries. The term OCIs refers to short, preliminary screening interviews conducted away from an employer's premises, usually on the university campus.[3] For law school OCIs, each pre-screening interview lasts about twenty minutes and is conducted by one or two representatives of a law firm. If the interview goes well, the law firm will call you to arrange for a full interview at the law firm's offices.

History of the Toronto OCIs

In the past, second-year summer recruitment in Toronto occurred during the winter term of second-year law school. Students would apply for a summer job once they received their fall-term grades and would interview in February, either during or close to reading week. The format of the interviews was virtually identical to the format of other recruitment programs (either articling interviews or first-year summer student interviews).

In 1997, it was clear that there was a growing trend for US (predominantly New York) law firms to recruit Canadian law students for second-year summer jobs through on-campus interviews. In 1998, the Law Society of Upper Canada, which is the regulatory body in Ontario for all law student recruitment in the province, moved second-year summer recruitment in Toronto from the winter term to the fall term of second-year study so that the Toronto law firms could remain competitive with New York recruitment. For two years, the recruitment of second-year summer students occurred in the fall term. It operated in the same manner as it had in the winter term, but without any OCIs.

In 2000, the Law Society of Upper Canada further extended the Toronto second-year summer student recruitment regulations to allow for OCIs. OCIs have retained their original format since their inception. Every year, new law firms and offices choose to participate in OCIs and there appears to be a trend towards this practice continuing for quite some time.

Overview of the OCI Process

Toronto law firms now travel across Canada in the fall term, conducting on-campus interviews at many law schools. Depending on the school you attend, OCIs can take place over one or two days, either in late September or in October.

Each law school sets up its interviews slightly differently, but all law schools provide their students with ample information about how the system operates. Most law schools conduct their OCIs in one large room sub-divided into small booths. The booths are placed side-by-side and are usually divided using drapes. The booths have a table and three chairs —one for the student and two for the interviewers. Some firms bring their brochures or other small gifts to give out to the students that they interview.

---

3   Because of the unusual format of OCIs, many law schools hold their OCIs off campus, either at a convention centre or large hotel where there is enough space to set up the interview booths.

Most law schools prepare a map of the large room, indicating the location of each booth so as to reduce confusion on the part of students.

Students interview in OCI time slots that are set up back-to-back, generally every twenty minutes. Some law schools hold eighteen-minute interviews with a two-minute break between each interview. The break allows students time to freshen up before their next interview and firms time to review their notes between interviews. Because there can be over twenty interview slots scheduled back-to-back in one day, falling behind in an interview timetable can produce chaotic results. To avoid falling behind, many law schools run the OCIs on very a very precise timetable, sometimes using stop watches and early notification systems to inform students and interviewers that an interview time slot is about to come to an end. Most law schools have food or lunch available for students and firm representatives. Also, there is usually a place for students to sit and read the newspaper or do a bit of homework between interviews.

Even though OCIs are not full interviews (they are classified as pre-screening interviews), they are nonetheless fairly formal. This formality means that it is appropriate for students to wear business attire (either a suit or a business-casual outfit) for these interviews.

Each law school will provide its students with OCI advice close to the actual event and will probably run a seminar or a lecture with advice and tips on summer interviews. In many cases, law schools will invite law firm representatives, or third-year students who went through the process the year before, to provide advice and answer questions. Frequently, law schools will also either run an interview workshop or practise the students' interview skills in private, mock-interview sessions. It is wise to keep track of this very helpful programming and to try to attend a mock interview.

In 2003, the Documentary Channel broadcast a documentary about OCIs called *The Genuine Article: The First Trial.*[4] Most law schools have a copy of this documentary on VHS in their library or career services office. It is well worth the viewing time for a student to watch it before she participates in OCIs. The documentary provides a very useful look at how OCIs operate from the perspective of a law firm and from the perspectives of three law students, each of whom is from a different school. It shows how the OCI booths are set up and how the interviews are conducted. It also shows the entire decision-making process for the follow-up interviews at the law firms. Most importantly, the documentary offers personal insights into various pressures and stressors that accompany this unique type of recruitment program.

OCI Regulations

As with other recruitment programs for the City of Toronto, OCIs and second-year summer recruitment are highly regulated by the Law Society of Upper Canada. As

---

4   *The Genuine Article: The First Trial.* Director: David Bezmozgis. Producers: Judy Holm and Michael McNamara. (Toronto, 2003: Markham Street Films Inc.)

many as forty law firms (including some government offices) may participate in OCIs and as many as seven hundred law students across Canada will apply every year to these law firms for second-year summer positions. Students are entitled to apply to as many firms as they choose and some students choose to apply to all firms. This means that there can be in excess of 15,000 applications processed each year within the whole recruitment program. As a result, it is very important that all who are involved abide by the regulations, especially the timing deadlines. Accommodations can be sometimes made for a particular student's situation, but most accommodations need to be discussed well in advance of OCIs and, depending on the situation, may require prior approval by the Law Society of Upper Canada.

The dates that applications are due, that law firms may contact students, that interviews may be held and that offers may be made, are all regulated by the Law Society. These dates change slightly every year. Your law school's career services office will post these dates well in advance for students. Some law schools, especially the out-of-province and regional schools, will offer to collect their students' applications in advance of the application deadline and will courier them in packages to the law firms in order to reduce mailing costs for their students.

Not all Canadian law schools run OCI programs, but all students are nonetheless entitled to apply for the jobs that are offered. Students in schools that do not run OCIs who are granted an interview with a law firm will meet the law firm for the first time at the full, in-firm interview. They will not have met the firm previously in a twenty-minute OCI. In these situations, the firm will be careful to ensure that the students are on equal footing with students whose schools held OCIs.

For law schools that organize OCIs, the career services office will advise the students as to which Toronto law firms are conducting OCIs and which Toronto law firms are participating in fall recruitment, but are not conducting OCIs. It is important for students not to come to conclusions about the quality of a law firm based on whether it conducts OCIs. For smaller and boutique practices, it is not necessarily cost effective to travel across Canada and meet students in a pre-screening interview. Instead, many of these law firms will ask for short writing samples from students in order to better distinguish between applicants.

After OCIs: The Full Interview

If a law firm is impressed with a student's on-campus interview, the firm may contact the student on a specified day (known colloquially as "call day") to arrange for a traditional in-firm interview. In-firm interviews are scheduled during a specified interview week and take from one and a half to two hours. During an in-firm interview, a student may meet several lawyers and may be given a tour of the law firm's premises. Some firms invite a student to return for a second interview if they are particularly interested in that student.

Most law firms participating in OCIs will hold a reception one evening during the interview week so that the students will be able to meet the firm's lawyers in a slightly more casual and social setting. Some law firms may even invite students to a lunch or a dinner where there may be other law students and lawyers. Both of these events, even though they take place in social settings, are still part of the interview process and students should remain professional at all times.

About Bay Street

Bay Street is a general term used to describe the offices located in the financial district in downtown Toronto. In the legal profession, the term *Bay Street firms* usually refers to the large national law firm practices that operate within the downtown Toronto financial district. Increasingly, the term *Bay Street firms* has come to include the smaller boutique practices that are also located in this same district.

For those who are not familiar with the Toronto downtown core and the financial district, it is worthwhile to look at a map and become familiar with the streets. Generally speaking, the financial district is bound by Queen Street West (to the north), Front Street (to the south), University Avenue (to the west), and Yonge Street (to the east). Almost of all of the law firms that interview second-year summer students through OCIs are located within these boundaries. The streets are set up in a standard grid pattern and you can easily walk from one end of the district to the other within about fifteen minutes.

It is not advisable to drive into the financial district for several reasons. First, parking is difficult to find and very expensive. Second, there is almost always heavy traffic and there are frequent traffic jams, even in parking lots. Third, there are many one-way streets and no-turn signs, so it is very difficult to manoeuvre through these streets if you are not familiar with them.

Busses and streetcars operate throughout the downtown core and there are five TTC subway stops on the perimeter of the financial district (Queen, King, Union, St. Andrew, and Osgoode stations). Taxis are also fairly easy to hail, both day and night, but they can sometimes take longer than walking to your destination within the financial district, depending on traffic conditions. It is wise to wear comfortable shoes on interview days because you will probably be on your feet from early morning to late at night. You will be walking from one interview to another, you will be walking through the firms themselves, and, later on, you will be standing at the cocktail parties.

One of the trickiest aspects of the financial district involves the names of the buildings. Because the office towers are so well known to Torontonians, law firms frequently use the buildings' names instead of their street addresses for mailing information. Also, many of these building are so large that they take up entire city blocks and have entrances from several streets. First Canadian Place, the TD Towers, Scotia Plaza, BCE Place, and Royal Bank Plaza are a few of the building names that leave students without geographic reference points. To make matters more confusing, the office towers are all linked in an underground maze of shopping concourses and pathways. Until you are accustomed to the financial district, it is almost certain that you will get lost or turned around in the underground system. Stay above ground if at all possible, even if it means wearing a jacket and carrying an umbrella.

It is worthwhile to wander through the financial district and locate the office towers, if possible, in advance of your interview days. It is also very important that you leave enough time between interviews to find your way to the next building and as well as up the elevators.

OCI Preparatory Research

One of the most important aspects of a law firm is the lawyers who work there. In the opinion of some, there is nothing more important for a student or new associate than working with skilled lawyers who provide good exposure to the law as well as exposure to interesting and diverse client files. When you are researching firms, take a look at the lawyers, including their practice areas. Find out whether they are publishing or teaching as adjunct faculty, whether they are writing articles in journals, or whether they are speaking to the profession. You ought to seek out lawyers who will act as mentors when you are interviewing for a summer job. The salary, the health club membership, and the window office are all ancillary issues and distractions from the main research you are conducting when you meet with each firm during in-firm interviews. Much of your preparatory research on a firm's lawyers can be done using websites and your library. Cross-reference lawyers' names with journal articles in your library and cases on Quicklaw or Westlaw. Many law firms post their lawyers' publications and recent cases on their websites, so it is quite easy nowadays to conduct this type of research.

OCI-Specific Resumés and Cover Letters

Toronto law firms that conduct OCIs across Canada each report receiving between six and seven hundred applications for second-year summer positions. Depending on the turn-around timetable, some of these firms have less than two weeks to read through all the applications and decide who to meet for an OCI. In many firms, the director of recruitment reads every single application. This procedure means that one person may be processing more than fifty applications a day during the first vetting. At this rate, the recruiters become experts at identifying small errors and form letters.

Because of the high volume of applications and the short time period in which the OCI firms must review all the applications, the standard for your resumé and cover letter clearly needs to be one of perfection. Refer to the section entitled "Resumés and Cover Letters" on pages 1–8 for help in this area. Remember that proofreading is exceptionally important. You must leave yourself plenty of time for this task.

Avoid leaving anything in your cover letter that indicates that you are operating a mail-merge program on your computer to write these letters. This is a stylistic point as well as a substantive point. Be cautious about confusing quantity for quality. Mail-merge programs can really do a lot of damage to your applications because if you have one unnoticed error in your template letter, you will have the same the error in all of your letters. Also, every year there are stories of a student who changes the name of the firm in the address line, but forgets to change the firm name in the body of his letter. If a firm sees this type of error, they immediately question whether the content of the letter was genuinely meant for them. Other commonly overlooked mistakes include pairing a recruitment director's name with the wrong firm, using incorrect gender titles (e.g., Mr. instead of Ms.), and listing practice areas that the firm does not offer. Letters that begin with "To Whom It May Concern" are not appropriate for these law firms, even though they may be acceptable in other cities.

Even though OCI law firms know that you are probably applying to several firms for a summer job, they still expect you to conduct research about each of the offices to which you apply. As difficult as it may seem to differentiate between full-service law firms, the expectation is that you should be able to communicate why you are interested in a particular firm and why the firm is different from the next office on the list. In order to gain this type of insight, it is important to know the areas of law that are practised at the firm (as well as the areas that they do not cover), some of the names of the lawyers, and some of the prominent clients of the law firm. Most of this information is available on websites and in the many law profession magazines and newspapers that are circulated in law schools.

Other Second-Year Summer Jobs

There are always a significant number of students who do not pursue, or do not obtain, summer jobs in law offices. Here are some useful suggestions to help you find a good, alternative second-year summer job:

1. **Look for Law School Postings.** Law schools are often the largest employer of law students when it comes to summer jobs. Law schools offer research assistant positions with professors; administrative positions in the library, student services, and alumni offices; legal aid positions; a host of jobs in the many projects in which the school is involved (e.g., innocence projects); and jobs in centres operated by the school (e.g., centres for innovation, family mediation centres). Seek out postings for positions in areas that overlap with your articling preferences. Law schools offer excellent summer jobs that law offices like to see on a student's resumé when the student applies for articling positions. Many law school positions are part-time and have flexible timetables, especially the research assistant positions. This flexibility enables students to take on more than one job during the summer.

2. **Look for Field-related Positions.** Whatever your law interests happen to be, there are great jobs that are connected to your area of law. For example, if you are interested in becoming a criminal defence lawyer, consider working for law enforcement organizations such as the county jail, the police station, or a parole board. If you are interested in entertainment law, consider working for a music label, a sports organ-

ization, a theatre, or any other business connected to the entertainment industry. The experience you gain will offer you insight into your future clients' businesses and will help to generate conversation during your articling interviews. Work with your career services office to produce a list of fields that are related to your law interests.

3. **Take on Two Jobs.** If you are having difficulty finding a full-time summer position in a law office or in an organization related to your area of interest, consider getting a regular summer job that pays the bills (e.g., as a waiter, bartender, or salesperson) and volunteer, or seek out a short internship, in a law-related organization. For instance, if you are interested in family law, volunteer at a women's crisis hotline. If you are interested in constitutional law, volunteer for a lobby group that obtained intervenor status on your favourite *Charter* case. Remember, all you need is about a week of volunteer experience in order to gain useful experience that you will be able to learn from and discuss during your articling interviews. If you choose this route, it is important that you do not mislead the interviewer as to the extent of your experience.

4. **Fill Gaps.** If you find that you have a number of summer jobs from which to choose, examine your current resumé and see if there are any gaps. If you have a lot of academic and retail experience, but you have never worked in an office, seek out an administrative position in an office. The experience will teach you how offices generally function. If you have a good deal of legal aid experience or you worked in a law office before you came to law school, consider taking on an academic summer job (e.g., a research assistantship, working for a law journal).

5. **Perform Outdoor Physical Labour.** If you cannot find a law or a law-related job, consider the benefits of taking a job that involves outdoor physical labour (e.g., landscaping, tree planting, construction). It is a healthy option and it will provide you with one last chance to work in an outdoor environment. Once you graduate from law school, you will be working indoors for the rest of your life. In addition, hard physical labour will teach you discipline and develop your stamina. This type of job will take an even greater toll on your body than articling. Hard physical labour will develop your endurance and provide good training for the long hours that will be required of you when you article. In your articling interview, you can make the case that punching a time clock at 6 a.m., taking orders from your foreman, and pushing your physical limits, was excellent preparation for a year of articles.

6. **Get More Education.** There are some summer course programs that can help you to become a more competitive candidate in particular fields. Note that a number of these programs will overlap with your school year. If you are interested in real estate law, consider getting your real estate license. If you want to pursue securities law, consider taking the securities course. If you have an interest in personal injury litigation, consider taking a CPR course, or even training as a paramedic, so as to learn more about emergency treatment. These courses will augment your legal

education in a very practical way and will help to make you a very attractive candidate for an articling position.

7. **Donate Your Time.** If you are in the fortunate position of not having to work to pay the bills, consider volunteering some of your time to help those in need. Food banks, drop-in centres, and elder community programs all need summer volunteers.

Whatever second-year summer job you find, remember to be proud of it during your articling interview. There is always something to be learned from a job. It is up to you to make the case as to how your summer job experience can be applied to your articling position.

$five$: **Third Year**

Beginning Your Articling Job Search

Primary Research

Before you embark on a job search, it is important to develop a plan. Working from a plan will keep you organized, help you manage your time, and ensure that you do not miss a stage. Every time you develop a new plan for a job search, you will become more efficient and, as a result, you will be more likely to achieve your goals. It will be helpful if you begin to make your plan by composing a list that identifies the key stages and components of your job search. This list will be similar to the type of list you will make when you embark on legal research on behalf of a client. Good research begins at your desk with a plan and a list.

1. **Career Services Resources.** For articling job research, your primary resources are likely to be any publications offered through your career services office. These publications include an articling handbook, a career guide, and a website with job postings, or printouts of job listings. These resources will be the foundation for your research. Surprisingly, there is no master list of all of the articling employers

throughout Canada. This is the case for most provinces as well. As a result, any list generated by your law school, or by you, will need to be supplemented with more independent research. If your law school does not have a formal career services office, it will probably have a student-run articling office with similar material.

2. **National Articling Database.** Another primary research tool for articling positions is the National Articling Database (NAD), hosted by LexisNexis Quicklaw. Your career services office or librarian can arrange for an instructional session on how to use this database. In most Canadian law schools, the information in the NAD database is reproduced in your career service office's publications because most of the Canadian law schools and Quicklaw seek out and share the bulk of articling recruitment information with each other. The benefits of the NAD are that you can track updated information beyond the publication date of your career services office's handbook and track historical information about past articling positions at the various offices.

Secondary Research

Once you have decided on your primary sources for research, it is wise to make a list of all the secondary materials that are available. Compiling this list of secondary materials is the more creative aspect of your research and the area that will differentiate you from other students. At this time, you will also tailor your research plan to fit your preferences.

1. **County Law Associations.** If you plan to look at positions that are outside major metropolitan areas, you may want to do a number of things. One course of action is to get in touch with all of the county law associations in the jurisdiction where you are seeking a job. Attempt to purchase a member's directory (increasingly, they are free to the public and available on-line) so that you can see the names of the offices that operate in the region, county, or smaller city. Then, get in touch with some of the lawyers on the list and ask them if they know who hires articling students in town. In the smaller jurisdictions, business is sometimes best conducted by word of mouth. There may be only a handful of offices that hire articling students each year and most lawyers will know the names of those offices. If you get in touch with any lawyer in Kingston, for instance, he may be able to refer you to the offices in the city that are known to hire articling students.

2. **White, Yellow, and Blue Pages.** Another thing you can do if you are interested in articling outside a major metropolitan area is to refer to a telephone directory for the city that appeals to you. You will have to review the white pages, the yellow pages, and the blue pages (listing government offices) of the telephone book. When using the white pages, you can search through the business pages if you know the names of the law offices. If you do not know the names of the law offices, you may have an easier time looking under Lawyers in the yellow pages.

3. **Alumni Directories.** Most law schools have some sort of alumni directory that the alumni office may share with students or with the career services office. This directory will provide a listing of where the law school's alumni are working. There are sometimes privacy issues with this directory, so the law school may not be able to share the entire list with its students; however, if you want to practise in a smaller city such as Banff, your alumni office may be able to help you find alumni there.

4. **Chambers of Commerce.** Another thing you can do if you are interested in smaller cities is to contact the chamber of commerce in the city that appeals to you. The chamber of commerce will provide you with the names of business organizations in the city. It will be especially helpful if you are looking for an in-house counsel position within the city. Also, you will typically find that lawyers are members of the board of the chamber of commerce and they may be willing to offer suggestions to you or provide you with information about the legal profession in the city.

5. **Courthouse Libraries.** If you are interested in articling in smaller jurisdictions, consider visiting the main civil or criminal courthouse, depending on what type of law interests you. Once you have wandered through the building and have read every notice on the walls, try to find the library inside the courthouse. In almost every main courthouse across Canada there is usually a law library for the lawyers and judges. These libraries are often run by the law association of the district. Introduce yourself to the librarian and explain that you are a law student looking for an articling job in the city (or district as the case may be). The librarian may be able to direct you to some law firms or introduce you to some lawyers who are working in the library at the time. Some libraries will allow students to put up a notice on the bulletin board indicating that they live in Welland or Bracebridge and are looking for an articling position in the region. This local approach is a very effective way to search for a job in a smaller community.

6. **Bar Associations.** Another route you can follow is to join the county's or province's bar association. The bar association is different from the law society in a province. The former is a voluntary professional association and the latter is a regulatory body. Their programming and functions frequently appear to overlap and it is not uncommon for students to get them confused; however, remember that they are separate and should be separately researched. Most bar associations have inexpensive, reduced rates for law students. If you know the area in which you want to practise, joining a bar association will provide an excellent opportunity to target law firms. For example, if you know you want to practise family law in Ontario, join the Ontario Bar Association and then sign up for the Family Law subsection. You will receive their e-mail postings concerning upcoming conferences and emerging issues. From these notices, you will learn the names of the lawyers who are specialists in family law in Ontario. If you attend one of the programs as a member, you will be able to meet and network with lawyers who practise family law exclusively.

In some jurisdictions, especially the larger urban centres (Toronto, Vancouver, and Calgary) and capital cities (Ottawa, Victoria, Edmonton, Regina, Winnipeg, Fredericton, Halifax, Charlottetown, and St. John's), the county or provincial bar association is possibly the best resource you can access for specialty practices.

7. ***The Canadian Law List.*** *The Canadian Law List* is a large, red book that can be found in every law library and in most career services offices. It is also available on-line. This resource has listings of the names of lawyers across Canada. Each entry includes the city and the name of the office where a lawyer is currently working. Because *The Canadian Law List* lists law firms as well as individual lawyers, you can easily find out the names of the lawyers working at each firm. Another excellent feature of *The Canadian Law List* is that it is divided up according to city and province, allowing you to target your research and focus directly on the city that interests you.

8. **Directories of Lawyers.** Most law school libraries and career services offices will have a directory of lawyers (published annually), at least for the province in which their law school is located. If you know a lawyer, he may have one on his desk that he will share with you. For example, there are a number of Ontario lawyers directories available, both on-line and in book form. These directories list the names, telephone numbers, and addresses of lawyers across Ontario in alphabetical order. They provide the name of the firm where each lawyer works, a current e-mail address, and sometimes offer website information. Directories are very useful, especially if you are researching positions or lawyers and need to confirm current addresses, law firm names, and telephone numbers. Many of the directories for the various provinces are commercial publications and are not mandated by the law societies. For this reason, they do not contain comprehensive lists of all lawyers. On the other hand, they are often the most accurate directories for contact information.

9. **Law Societies.** Your province's law society's website is another area that you should bookmark and refer to frequently. You will visit this website many times, during your articling process, your bar ad process, and once you are called to the Bar as a lawyer. Each of these websites contains a vast amount of information because each is designed both for the public (clients) and the profession (lawyers). As a result, these websites can get very confusing and may require a bit more time to navigate than other websites. Some of these websites post articling positions that become available after the major recruitment for articling students has been completed. These websites are a very useful resource for third-year students who are searching for articling positions in September, once school has begun.

10. **Headhunter Websites.** Although the headhunter websites — ZSA, The Affiliates/ Robert Half, RainMaker, Marsden Nagata, and Life After Law, to name a few — do not typically post articling jobs, these websites allow you to see the firms that are currently in need of more lawyers. If you see that a firm is posting a position for a very junior associate, it may indicate that the firm is growing or building a junior practice.

11. **Case Law.** If you read an interesting recent case in class, take a look at the beginning of the judgment where the names of the lawyers who represented the plaintiff, respondent, or appellant (whatever the case may be) are listed under the style of cause. If you are impressed with a lawyer who has taken on a certain case, you can cross-reference her name using one of the lawyers directories and find out where she works. This will be harder to do for federal cases and Supreme Court of Canada judgments because you need to know the province of origin for the cases in order to cross-reference and find the lawyers' names in a directory. *The Canadian Law List* may be particularly helpful for these cases.

12. **Law Reports.** In most provinces, once you are called to the Bar, you will receive the province's law reports, either weekly or monthly, in an unbound format. Eventually, these law reports can be found in bound format in the law library (e.g., the *Alberta Reports, Ontario Reports, British Columbia Law Reports*). At the beginning of most of the unbound law reports, you will find various law society notices, professional announcements, and lists of upcoming programs for lawyers. From these announcements, you can find out the names of the lawyers who are leaders in their practice areas. They are the lawyers who are speaking at conferences and publishing new books. The law reports also contain notices of position vacancies for associate positions. It will be helpful, especially if you are interested in creating an articling position for yourself or going after a very small law firm, to find out what law firms are looking for junior associates because this may indicate a need for junior assistance at these offices. Unbound law reports can be found in your law library and possibly in your career services office (if someone in the office is a lawyer and receives them regularly). If you know a lawyer, you can ask him for his discarded copies once he has read through them for his practice.

13. **Industry Magazines and Newspapers.** The various law magazines and the legal newspapers (e.g., *Lexpert, National* magazine, *Canadian Lawyer*) can be found in all career services offices and will probably be archived in your library as well. These resources will help you to find out about lawyers who are leaders in certain areas of practice, new transactions and developments in the law, and current professional issues. Conveniently, there are also many advertisements placed by law firms, allowing you to learn the names of law firms that may not be in your law school's articling handbook or on the NAD.

14. **Archived Material.** Take a look at handbooks and listings for previous years. Most career services offices archive their material. If you want to find out the timing of job postings in the past, this might be a good research tool for you. The information is also available on the NAD.

15. **Non-Traditional Articling Options.** Several province's law societies now allow students to pursue non-traditional articling opportunities. In Ontario, for instance, the Law Society of Upper Canada permits international articles, allowing a student to

article up to six months in another jurisdiction anywhere in the world and get cred-it for it towards Ontario articles. They also allow for joint articles during which an articling student splits his or her time between two offices. In addition, part-time articles are now allowed in Ontario for those who have parenting or other obliga-tions. Finally, there is an opportunity to have an abridgement of articles if, for instance, you are already a lawyer in another jurisdiction. In each of these situa-tions — international articles, joint articles, part-time articles, and abridgements — a student must obtain prior approval from the Law Society of Upper Canada before the articling term begins. Many other provinces have developed, or are developing, similar non-traditional options.

Organizational Advice

1. **Files.** Keep a file during your articling job search. Buy file folders or accordion files, whatever you prefer. Keep everything, including your notes, until after you are called to the Bar and have a job as an associate. You should keep a record of each cover letter that you send to an office and you should keep a record of all of the research that you have done because it might come in handy a couple of years down the road. This process is similar to the way in which you will organize your work when you are a lawyer in a practice. There are a lot of similarities between conduct-ing an articling job search and working on a file as a lawyer.

2. **Share.** Share your research with your friends. Because there is such a high volume of information that you need to go through, you may want to sit down in groups of two or three and share the information that each of you has acquired. When you are a lawyer, you may find it useful to share information in this manner with other lawyers.

3. **Contacting Law Offices.** If there are certain offices in which you are very interested, consider telephoning the articling students at these offices before they finish their articling terms. Ask them some questions. They may provide you with a key piece of information about the office that you will want to refer to in your cover letter.

    Remember, any time you engage in communication with an office you should consider it to be part of your interview and application process. You should employ all of your diplomatic skills and take into account that lawyers and articling stu-dents are very busy. Contact only one person per law office, unless that person directs you to someone else within the office. Leave a polite voice-mail message if you do not reach the lawyer or student. Always introduce yourself as a law student and give your full name and the name of the law school you are attending. Most law firms have call display and it would be inappropriate to keep calling a lawyer's direct line until someone answers the telephone. Voice mail is very effective. If a lawyer or student does not return your message, try not to badger them. Instead, speak to your career services office about other contacts or leads they may be able to suggest. Frequently, lawyers are in the middle of a court case or a file and do not have the time to return all of their telephone calls immediately.

4. **E-mail.** If you e-mail an office, send one e-mail at a time. Do not send the same e-mail to more than one person within an office. Ensure your e-mail address is professional and your message is short, direct, and professional. Try not to ask for a lawyer's personal opinion in an e-mail since most lawyers are hesitant to put their opinions in writing. Instead, ask the lawyer a factual question (remember to ensure that the answer is not available on the law firm website) and politely inquire as to whether you can contact her by telephone. When speaking to you on the phone, a lawyer may be more inclined to offer candid advice and may even offer to meet you for coffee. Also, remember that the lawyer may make notes about this contact (especially a lawyer working at a larger firm) and these notes may be added to a file or a database. For this reason, make sure that your behaviour and your questions are professional. Finally, remember that senior lawyers and some very small offices may not favour e-mail as a means of communication. In these cases, an unanswered e-mail may be a signal to switch to the telephone.

5. **Second Applications.** If you applied to an office for a summer position and you plan to reapply to the same office for an articling position, remember that the law firm (especially large national offices) may remember your summer application or may have kept your summer application in a file. For this reason, it is a wise idea to change your cover letter when applying for the articling position. When the firm opens up your file, your letter will demonstrate to them that you are serious about applying to them and that you are not simply circulating the same application from the previous year. Also, you will have learned a lot more about your preferences in the months between summer applications and articling applications, so it will be natural to have developed a new cover letter.

6. **Merge Programs.** Avoid mail-merge letters and mail-merge e-mails. There are a number of reasons for doing so. Sometimes there are formatting problems with merge programs. Also, if you have one error in a letter, you will produce thirty letters with the same error when you use a mail-merge program. It is really not in your interest to use a mail-merge program in your articling job search. In addition, the use of mail merge does not conceptually match how you should be approaching these law offices. Even though mail merge may make your system easier, your aim is to treat each of the law offices individually, just as you want them to treat you as an individual. It is important that students do not sacrifice the quality of each individual application so that they can send out a large quantity of applications with ease. While you may be sending off a great number of articling applications, it is important not to let the law firms figure out that you are doing so.

7. **Timing of Job Postings.** Another thing to keep in mind is that not all of the articling positions come up at the same time as the articling positions offered through for-

mal recruitment programs. There are some offices that hire late, once you are back at school and in your third year. They are smaller offices that do not necessarily know early on whether they will have the budget or the workload to hire someone. Offices that break away from other law firms and new, start-up offices also tend to hire late. As well, some government offices are prevented from hiring students until either the federal or provincial budgets are passed down. If you want to identify offices that typically hire students late in the cycle, ask your career services office if you can read through the late-hiring articling postings from previous years.

8. **Know Your Rules.** You should read the rules for every articling recruitment program you intend to take part in. Each province is very different and sometimes each city within a province will have a different articling recruitment timetable. Sometimes these rules are drawn up by the province's law society, provincial bar association, or county law association. In some provinces, such as Ontario, there are overlapping rules. In these cases, the province's law society will set general rules for cities and then an individual city will define a set of sub-rules. Such is the case for Hamilton, London, and Ottawa. There are many rules regarding deadlines, beginning with application deadlines and continuing through to interviews and offers. Understanding these rules is the key to navigating successfully through the articling process. As a lawyer, you always operate on behalf of your clients by knowing the rules of a process before you begin it.

9. **Summer Students at Law Firms.** Students who have already secured a summer job and plan on returning to the same office for articling will probably not have to re-interview with the firm for the articling job. Each office has a different method for notifying its students about hire-backs. Sometimes the law society or bar association sets regulations or guidelines that state when a firm should notify its summer students about their articling positions. It is always wise to take a bit of time to research other articling opportunities that are available. Every year, there are some students who find that they do not like the firm they selected for the summer for a variety of reasons. They may wish to switch cities, practice areas, or to a law firm of a different size. Also, there are occasionally situations where things just do not work out and the firm does not invite you to article with them. Make sure you are prepared to deal with a situation of this nature: have a backup plan. Remember, this is how you will work as a lawyer: with a solid secondary plan in case your primary plan falls through.

The foundation of a solid articling job search is built on diversification at its outset. You ought to keep your search broad when you begin your research, but you should be able to target what you are doing by the final stages of your research, when you are ready to write your cover letters.

Articling in Another Province

Many students choose to study law in a province that is not the province they originally came from. Other students study law in a province that is not the province in which they intend to practise law. Many students do not know where they will practise and plan to decide during law school. Recently, the law societies have developed interprovincial agreements to make it easier to move from one province to another as a lawyer once you are called to the Bar.

When you are deciding on the province where you want to summer or article, you are really deciding where you want to practise, at least for the first few years after you are called to the Bar. Most law firms spend a lot of money on their summer and articling programs and are therefore unlikely to find a candidate attractive if they do not get the impression that the candidate intends to live in the city for at least several years. If you are wondering what the Atlantic Ocean is like in the summer, but you are from Vancouver and plan on practising in BC, participating in cross-border recruitment through your law school is probably not the best way for you to visit Halifax.

If you are seeking an articling position in a province other than the province that you come from, or in a province other than the province where you are attending law school, you will benefit from placing an emphasis on your interest in the new city and province when you speak to the firms. Depending on where you are studying, consider discussing your interest in the city or province in your cover letter. For instance, a student who plans to return to the city that he is from when he finishes law school could write, "I am from Winnipeg. I was accepted at Osgoode Hall Law School, but I plan on returning to Winnipeg." It is likely that a statement of this nature is all that is necessary. A different student might write, "I am from Windsor and I am studying law in Victoria, but I am intrigued by federal issues and intend to move to Ottawa to practise law." This student stands a good chance of persuading firms that she is committed to living in Ottawa and that she wishes to start out her career in a city that is altogether new to her. Yet another student might write, "Although, I am originally from Saskatchewan, I am attending the University of Alberta and plan on remaining here permanently." This student is likely to have said enough about his intentions when it comes to Edmonton articling applications. Finally, be sure to bring up your interest in living in a new city or province during an interview, even if the interviewer does not raise the topic.

Students who can communicate their long-term intentions will be able to allay any *flight risk* concerns that a law firm may have when reading an out-of-province application. A law firm that reviews hundreds of articling applications needs to understand why you should be considered a serious candidate when your employment record or your study record does not indicate a connection to their city. To communicate your intentions effectively, you must be direct, forthright, and keep the explanation relatively simple. There are many good reasons as to why students seek jobs in other provinces. Some need to move for family reasons, such as a spouse obtaining a position in another city. Others are more mobile and will move to the location where the best job is offered. Some wish to move to a different environment — drawn by the climate, the size of the city, or by some other attraction (e.g., access to skiing in Calgary and Vancouver). Others wish to move for a romantic reason (e.g., a student who falls in love with an out-of-province student during law school). All of these are legitimate reasons for seeking an articling position in another province or city and do not require you to go into too many personal details.

When applying for a position in another province, it is important to indicate the cities where you have worked on your resumé. This practice will help to inform the interviewer about the various locations that your studies and travels have taken you.

If you are looking for an out-of-province articling position, consider speaking to the alumni office of your law school to see if there are alumni who work in the city where you are applying for articles. Alumni in other cities sometimes form chapters and networks and they may be a very helpful resource when it comes to connecting you with law firms in a city. Also, consider chatting with faculty members who are from different parts of the country.

When applying for an articling position outside the province where you are attending law school, it is your responsibility to learn about the recruitment regulations, including deadlines and filing obligations for bar admissions programs. This information is now available on most law society websites. Most provinces and territories can be researched with relative ease, but the process requires some patience. Because some provinces' recruitment programs schedule deadlines that are months ahead of other provinces' deadlines, it is important to discuss your articling plans with your career services office relatively early in your second year. Some second-year summer recruitment programs are hiring mechanisms for articling students, either informally (as with the Toronto OCI firms), or formally (as in the Atlantic provinces), so it may be wise to connect your summer job search with your articling plans. Most career services offices will assist students in finding information and may even have copies of the regulations for other provinces since many of the law school career services offices exchange articling handbooks as a courtesy to one another. You may even be able to purchase a copy of an articling handbook from a law school in the province where you intend to article. The articling handbook will be a valuable resource for you.

six: **Articling**

How to Excel at Articles

Articling is a hard year, regardless of your background. It may be the first time you have ever had to push yourself beyond your personal limits. Few lawyers recall their articling year with pleasure; however, almost every lawyer will tell you that what she learned during articling shaped her lawyering skills.

There are several factors that increase pressure during articling and each factor should be addressed individually as you move though the articling experience. First, there is the translation of your academic understanding of the legal system into a practical application of service to clients. The apprenticeship model that is the basis for articling pre-dates university law training. Some argue that the amount of learning that occurs during articling equals or exceeds the amount of learning that occurs during the three years of a university law degree. When articling, you must absorb a tremendous amount of new information within a relatively short period of time. If you were involved in your law school's legal aid program or you were a law clerk before attending law school, you may find the transition from law school to articling easier.

A second factor that increases the pressure during articling is the volume of work. Many lawyers recall that the heavy work load was the most difficult aspect of articling. In the illustration below, the work volume is represented by a triangle made up of three elements.

Volume of Work:

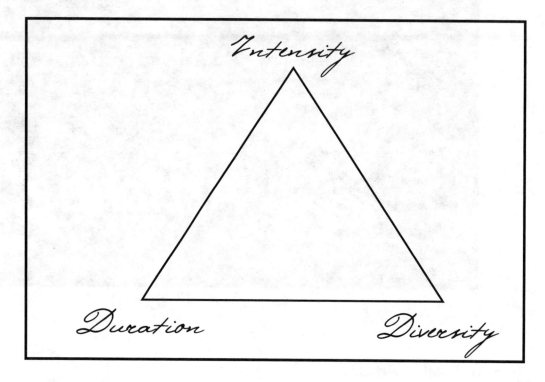

Most articling programs are designed to develop a student's lawyering skills through the duration, diversity, and intensity, of the work load. The most frequently talked about aspect of articling is the duration of the work day and work week. Simply put, there is a great deal of work and sometimes it seems as if there is too much to do. The diversity of the work is usually mandated by the province's law society to ensure that the articling student experiences a wide range of client services. The intensity of the work is linked to the student's realization that his legal research or other legal work on a file directly affects his client's case. It is easy to study the issues relevant to a motion for summary judgment, but it is hard to apply these issues so that you are successful in achieving or defending a summary dismissal of your client's case.

To succeed as an articling student, you ought to prepare yourself for all three aspects of the work load. The student who expects to work a long day, who expects diverse files, and who understands that intensity is a part of being a lawyer, will be better prepared to adapt to the learning environment of an apprenticeship.

A third factor that increases the pressure during articling is the performance and evaluation aspect of the apprenticeship experience. Unlike law school, where students are evaluated on the basis of an exam or an essay at the end of a course, the articling year is a system involving constant performance and constant evaluation. This system of evaluation is more comparable to a coaching environment than a formal teaching environment. As an apprentice, it is very important that you take the feedback you receive seriously, absorb it quickly, and improve accordingly. Some of the feedback you receive will contain elements of criticism; a good student will react positively to this criticism.

The following are some thoughts and ideas on how to address the factors that increase pressure during your articling experience.

Behave Like a Lawyer Now

In the United States, students graduate from law school and, after passing the bar admissions exams, become first-year associates. In the Canadian system, articling is a buffer period after law school, but this system does not entitle a Canadian law graduate to continue to behave as if he were a student once he is working in a law office. The public expects your office behaviour to match the behaviour of the lawyers in the office, just as the public expects residents in a hospital to behave the same way that doctors behave. One of the most important things to remember is that you must not speak about your clients' cases or identify your clients outside of the office. Client confidentiality is at the core of the legal system and must be observed by all, including articling students. If your client's files appear on the front pages of the newspapers, you are not allowed to announce to friends that you are working on the transaction unless it is publicly known that your firm is involved. Even if this is the case, you are not permitted to provide commentary on the situation. Such leaks can, and have, spoiled transactions.

Expect a Long Day and a Long Week

You should expect your articling experience to be your primary focus for the year and make plans accordingly. This is probably not the best year to subscribe to the opera or join a hockey team; you cannot expect to be able to attend all of the performances or games. Try to adapt to the long work day and long work week. It might help to join a gym near your office rather than using a gym near your home after work. If you work out before you get into the office or during lunch, you can stay at the office past 5 p.m., if necessary, and still get some exercise. It might be helpful to rent an apartment close to the office so that you can avoid lengthy daily commutes in traffic and easily get into work on a Saturday or Sunday.

Maintain and Preserve Your Energy Levels

The articling year is comparable to running a marathon. You cannot sprint a marathon, nor can you perform at a high energy level throughout your entire articles. Eat well to maintain your energy and allow yourself time for rest and leisure when you leave the office. Remember to pace yourself so that you can handle the long hours required to complete the heavy workload.

Take Vacations

Most articling programs in Canada offer at least two weeks of vacation. Try to take these two weeks if possible. A vacation will boost your energy levels, offer you some much-needed distance from your files, and give you a rest from the daily grind of working in an office. Most importantly, a vacation will refresh your attitude and alleviate the sense of frustration that can develop when starting a new job. If you article with a firm where there are rotations through different departments, try to take the vacation in the last week of a rotation rather than in the middle, or at the beginning, of a new rotation. The timing will help to minimize the disruption of the work schedules of both you and your principal lawyers.

Always Be Nice

Surprisingly, some articling students think that being a lawyer allows them to boss the staff around. Remember that even though you have three years of law school training, the staff have far more experience working in a law office than you do and will resent having to deal with a student who does not treat them respectfully. The secretaries, clerks, librarians, bookkeepers, and other support staff in a law firm are part of your educational infrastructure and you will benefit greatly if you treat them the same way you wish to be treated by the lawyers.

Remain Dispassionate

A good lawyer advocates for her client, but does not step into the shoes of the client emotionally when dealing with his case. Emotion tends to cloud reason and logic and it is incumbent on lawyers to subordinate their emotional reactions, even in the most difficult and heart-wrenching cases. As frustrating and obstinate as the behaviour of some opposing counsel and opposing clients may seem to you, focus on the legal issues at hand and refrain from communicating emotion in your letters or during conversations with them.

Do Not Compete

If there is more than one articling student at your firm, remember to treat your co-articling students as colleagues, not competitors. Articling is not a race or a competitive game. Your principal lawyers are evaluating you on your individual ability. They are also evaluating you on your ability to work in a group because files frequently require many lawyers to work together to achieve the client's goals. If you are a fan of reality TV, *Eco-Challenge* offers a good example of how to work productively in a team. In *Eco-Challenge,* groups of four work together in an adventure race. All four team members must finish the race together for the team to succeed. Disputes and competition between team members weaken the team and threaten the goals of individual members. Successful teams almost invariably consist of members who work together harmoniously and who avoid emotional spats. The television show provides a good lesson for the workplace. You and your co-articling students will advance further if you help one another. Conversely, you will only weaken your chance of achieving your individual goals if you try to compete with other articling students. If you have extra time and you see another articling student burdened with work, offer to take over a file for him. He will return the favour when the situation is reversed. Also, share your legal research and precedents so that others may build on your work, rather than repeat what you have already done. You will conduct yourself in this manner when you are a lawyer working in a law firm.

Be Wary of Bad Advice

Because articling is such a new experience, some articling students adopt blanket theories such as, "if you want to get hired back, be sure to work for lawyer X," or, "never leave the office before 7 p.m." This type of quasi-superstitious advice distracts students from the truth. If you want to get hired back, seek out work from as many lawyers as possible so that you experience a wide range of files and different lawyering styles. Likewise, if there is work to be done, stay until it is done, but certainly leave if you have completed your work for the day. Remember that there are no secret short cuts to articling and be wary of advice based on such generalizations.

Discuss Your Workload

If you have extra time, let your mentor know that you are available for more work. If you are pressed for time and you are concerned that you may not meet all your deadlines, speak to your mentor. It is your mentor's role to ensure that you have a balanced workload and assist you in prioritizing your work. If necessary, your mentor will speak to your assigning lawyers about competing or conflicting deadlines. Attempt to discuss your concerns about your workload with your assigning lawyer first. If you are concerned that you may not be able to complete an assignment before the deadline, tell your assigning lawyer so when he gives you the assignment. He may be able to give you precedents to speed up your work or he may even be able to extend the deadline a bit. He may also be willing to review the assignments he has already given you and help you to determine the assignments that should be focused on first.

Never Miss a Deadline

If you miss a deadline, speak immediately to the assigning lawyer and obtain instructions from her as to how to rectify the situation. This will be an unpleasant experience and it will deter you from missing deadlines in the future. Do not try to resolve the situation yourself. Missing a deadline may be a matter of solicitor's negligence if the deadline was a limitation period.

Review Your Law Society's Education Plan

Most provincial law societies require law firms to ensure that their articling students experience a certain range of legal work. A law firm must indicate that it will provide articling students with this range of legal experience in order to have its articling program approved. The description of legal work to be covered is sometimes referred to as an *education plan*. In most cases, the required range of legal work will be outlined in the material provided to you by your law society, or by your law firm, in advance or at the beginning of your articling year. Be sure to review the educational plan and add to it any other types of legal work that you want to cover during articling. Review the list several times with your mentor throughout your articling experience. Let your mentor know if there is legal work that you have not yet encountered but wish to experience during articling. Remember that articling is part of your education as a lawyer and it is important for you to be active in ensuring that you are receiving a good range of file experiences.

Seek Out Mentors, Not Confidantes

Your mentors, both the formal mentors assigned to you and lawyers who become your informal mentors, are there to guide and educate you. Avoid treating your mentors as confidantes. Do not discuss unimportant personal matters with them such as the stress of articling or the dynamics of relationships between articling students. For conversations of this nature, talk to friends outside of the firm. Most students regret engaging in personal conversations with professional colleagues, especially when the student has allowed emotion to dominate the conversation.

Accept Mundane Tasks With Grace

Occasionally, lawyers will ask students to perform seemingly mundane tasks, sometimes related to files and sometimes related to the lawyer personally. Most law societies discourage lawyers from assigning personal tasks to articling students. The days in which articling students collected dry cleaning for lawyers are long gone but occasionally a lawyer will ask a student to fight a speeding ticket for her or carry file boxes to the court house. Although tasks such as rearranging a file, photocopying, proofreading, and delivering documents may seem boring, they can still teach the student something. If your articling experience is dominated by these tasks, speak to your mentor. It is important to ensure that you are covering all the types work listed in your education plan. When it comes to the odd chore, accept it with grace and treat it with the same diligence as you would any other work you are given.

Docket Fully

One of the goals of an articling program is to train students in time management. To learn to manage your time, you must accurately document how long it takes you to do something. Later, you can reflect on your day and learn from your behaviour. Docketing, the method used by most private practice lawyers to bill for their time, offers you the ability to track the time you spend on each file and on each task. Some students are reluctant to put the full amount of time they spent on a file into their docket because they fear they took too long. For instance, if you took a week to draft a statement of claim after a lawyer suggested it should take a couple of days, be sure to put the full time spent on the drafting, regardless of the lawyer's estimate of the time it would take. There are a number of reasons as to why you should do so. First, lawyers frequently forget that articling students take twice to triple the amount of time that it would take a lawyer to do the task. Second, the lawyer can easily *write off* your time before the bill is sent to the client if she thinks you spent an excessive amount of time on the task. Third, your mentor may wonder why you are in the office for twelve hours a day when you are only docketing three hours of work. Include the full amount of time you spend on each file, analyze the efficiency with which you completed the task, and let the billing lawyer decide whether to include your full docket.

Read Before You Write

Because there is so much work to do, most students immediately attempt to perform a task assigned to them by a lawyer. Rather than rushing into a file, read parts of the client's file first. This practice may help to focus your work and make you more efficient when you are researching or drafting documents. For example, when you are assigned a memo, speak to the assigning lawyer to see if it is appropriate for you to spend an hour reading the file in order to help contextualize the research. Most lawyers will encourage you to review a file before you begin work on a new matter. The hour spent reviewing the file may save you over two hours of off-topic research. Reviewing a file, especially the correspondence brad, is quite educational; you will see how a lawyer frames and develops his client's case through letter writing.

Use Precedents and In-house Research Databases

If your firm has a precedent database or research database, consider starting most of your assignments by reviewing the contents of these databases. You can learn a lot from working with a trustworthy database document and then tailoring it to meet your client's situation. Depending on the level of detail provided by the precedent database, consider using precedents authored by your assigning lawyer so that you will capture her style and content preferences. For instance, if you are assigned the drafting of a commercial lease, look for previous commercial leases drafted by your assigning lawyer and use them as the basis for the current client's lease. If your law firm does not have a formal precedent database, ask the lawyer for a sample lease previously drafted by her on another file. She may guide you through the clauses of the sample lease in order to save you time and help you learn the procedure. If a lawyer asks you to draft a letter in her name, consider reading other letters written by the lawyer on the file so that you can adopt her style.

Read All Precedents

Be sure to read the whole document if working from, and editing, a precedent. It is essential that you understand all of the clauses of the documents you draft. You will learn a good deal if you ask questions about the meaning or effect of clauses.

Document All Legal Research

There are two things that students sometimes forget to document when they are researching the law: the date and their research paths. First, always add the date, including the year, to the file you are researching. Because the law changes and files are sometimes active for several years, it is important for future readers of your research notes to know when you were doing the research. Second, write down all of the research paths that you pursued (e.g., DLRs, CED, Abridgment, Quicklaw database ORP, Paciocco & Stuesser's *Law of Evidence*). Remember to indicate the keywords or phrases you used in each of your searches (e.g., "will challenge," "testamentary capacity," "estates"). Most importantly, do not forget to include places where you did not find anything. Documenting your research paths will ensure that you do not repeat an unhelpful search when you are updating your research. Keep your research notes in the file, as back-up documentation to your memo, in case your instructing lawyer wishes to review how you researched the issue.

Memo Writing

Memo writing will dominate the articling experience of some students. Keep in mind that memos are written in the style of business, not academic, writing. In business writing, the goal is efficiency and transparency. You must select the most accurate word and the most efficient phrase every time. Your clients and instructing lawyers should be able to read your memos in minutes, not hours. There are a number of tools you can use to facilitate clear and transparent writing. For example, the use of headings and numbering can improve the overall organization of your memo and make it easier for a reader to understand your message. Also, with business writing you must put your conclusions first. A good memo will have a summary of conclusions at the beginning of the memo, followed by a detailed explanation of these conclusions in the body of the memo. Be sure to ask your instructing lawyer how long she thinks the memo should be so that you can gauge the level of detail she is looking for. If a lawyer asks you to find two or three cases on a topic and prepare a short memo summarizing them, consider attaching the cases to the memo for her to review.

Follow Lawyers Around

Articling students can learn a good deal about lawyering techniques and style through observation. Listen to lawyers when they speak on the telephone with their clients, examine their letter writing and drafting styles, and watch them in court. Sometimes you may feel as if you are eavesdropping, but most lawyers will encourage you to tag along to meetings and court proceedings and listen in on their telephone conversations. Provided you do not risk missing a deadline on an assignment, it is worthwhile to take the time to watch lawyers at work. Your observations will give you a solid foundation upon which to develop your own personal style.

Reflect and Grow

After every rotation, or midway through though your articles if you do not have rotations, take some time to reflect on the areas you have excelled in during your articling experience. Attempt to understand why you performed so well. Was it because you handed things in the day before the deadline? Was it because you were more thorough than anyone else when dealing with a certain issue? Was it because you were able to pinpoint an issue or come up with a creative solution for a client? Or, was it because you really enjoyed that area of law or working with one particular lawyer? Whatever it was that allowed you to perform well, repeat it. Continue to develop these strengths. Also, try to understand what constraints prevented you from performing as well on other files. Reflection on your past performances is a key factor when it comes to achieving the rapid improvement that is needed to succeed at articling.

Advanced Memo Writing

By the time you reach the second half of your articling experience, you should be able to add more value to a file you are assigned than you could when you were in the first half of your articling experience. At this later stage in your development, your knowledge about how a file works will enable you to add a sentence on a proposed next move at the end of a memo. Express what you think the next step might be and offer to take the file to that next step. For example, you could write, "Based on the research, I do not believe that the client has a very good chance of success on summary judgment. Would you like me to draft mediation materials in the event the client instructs you to mediate the matter?" This example represents the thinking of a lawyer. Your ability to indicate that you understand the next stage will speak to the level of maturity you have attained through your work experience.

Evaluate the Firm

Just as the firm is evaluating whether you are suitable to become one of their associates, so should you be evaluating the firm's suitability as your employer. For the firm, it is a business decision whether to hire you back. For you, it is a personal decision. Evaluate your experience as an articling student and determine whether the firm suits your personal and professional goals. On that note, do not focus on getting hired back until about one month before the end of articling or it may consume your thought processes. Throughout articling, you should focus almost exclusively on the quality of your work and the growth of your knowledge, not on the prospect of being hired back. It is easy to say this, but it is a very hard thing to do. In the end, it is worthwhile to attempt to control your thoughts on this topic.

As serious as articling is, remember to sometimes look for the humorous side of things when you are with your fellow articling students. There are many office experiences that, if shown on a TV sitcom, would elicit genuine laughter. It is important to allow these moments to provide some comic relief in your life. The ability to see the humorous side of a situation will help you to take the inevitable small foul-ups and hair-pulling frustrations in your stride and will offer you an occasional lighter perspective on the articling process.

seven : **Associate Positions**

A Framework for an Associate Job Search

When you embark on an associate job search, it is quite different from embarking on an articling job search. An associate job search is more targeted than an articling job search because you have now acquired more information about yourself, the profession, and the market. As a result, you have a much more solid foundation upon which to build a job search plan.

When sending out associate job applications, consider sending out only a few applications at a time. It may no longer be strategic to send out fifty letters at once since this is no longer a formalized recruitment process and such methods may appear unfocused and unprofessional. You are at a stage in your career development that is more individualized and professional. You should now favour quality over quantity.

Develop Your Career Plan Early

The most important message to be emphasized when building an associate career plan is to start early. To begin with, students need take a very thoughtful, private approach to understanding themselves. Many students followed other people's suggestions when deciding to attend law school. Others just followed the next logical next step; perhaps they did not feel they had finished with their studies and were looking to extend their academic learning. Many entered law school because they had the grades to get in, but never really analyzed why they chose law school or what they expected from themselves and their degrees.

The longer you operate without a self-conscious understanding of what you really want out of your experiences and career, the less likely it is that you will be able to take control over your own career development and ensure that you are feeling productive and happy with your life.

When to Start Contacting Offices

When contacting offices for associate positions, your timing is very important, not just for the success of your job search, but for your own integrity, current job satisfaction, and consequent performance.

It is hard enough to article and be at work everyday, let alone if all your energy is spent on an underground job search. The risk that your office may find out that you are running a job search while articling is serious. Should your office find out that you are conducting a job search, it could jeopardize their long-term interest in you. A below board job search is difficult, both practically and emotionally. If you enjoy where you are working and would like to be hired back, you should focus on that goal exclusively and refrain from contacting any other offices until about a month before the end of your articles.

Keep a Journal on Yourself

Start a journal or open a file documenting what has happened to you over the past year. Mark down specific experiences that you had during articles (e.g., corporate mergers, IPOs, due diligence, trials, motions, examinations for discovery, real estate closings, different areas of legal research, memo writing, drafting agreements). Make note of the files you enjoyed working on and analyze why you found them intriguing and challenging. Also, mark down the types of files that you would prefer to avoid once you are called to the Bar.

At the same time, take a look at how your values have changed. Think about the people that particularly impressed you, whether it was a lawyer you worked for, opposing counsel that you met, clients, or other people in the law firm. Take note of the way they handle their careers and what they do that you do or do not admire. This process will help you choose a role model. The ability to observe and analyze is something you will always use as a lawyer. Hone these skills now for your own personal benefit, not just for your clients' benefit.

These days, it is unlikely that professionals will work at the same job for thirty-five years. Professionals move around in their careers and jobs much more than their parents did twenty or thirty years ago. You are more likely than not to embark on a job search process not once, but several times. Every time you go through the process, you will improve if you take the time to analyze what you did in your previous job search and what results your efforts yielded. Once you have performed this analysis, you can refine your search process. This type of analysis is similar to how you will refine your legal research skills as you progress from one file to another. Be sure to constantly observe yourself, observe the people around you, and develop a deliberate plan for yourself.

What to Look for in Your Job Search

What are you searching for when you look for a position? There are so many factors that the process can become overwhelming. Are you looking for money? Prestige? Status? Intellectual challenge? Location? Are there certain clients you wish to service or a certain area of law you wish to specialize in? All of these factors are valuable, but you must rank their value and priority according to what is important to you. This is a personal priority scale that should be developed privately, or with your spouse or life partner. Resist letting others tell you what should be important in your life, otherwise you might end up living someone else's life. If you let this happen, you will find yourself unhappy with your personal development as you pursue your career.

Find a Good Mentor

One of the most important elements to look for when you embark on an associate search is a good mentor. There is nothing more valuable than finding a mentor who is not only a good lawyer, but also a good human being. What you learn from an ethical, moral mentor will help you in any career, any culture, and across any jurisdiction. A good mentor is arguably more valuable than the extra money you may receive from another law firm that lacks good mentors.

It is becoming harder to find good mentors because in the last decade or two the practise of mentoring has ceased to be a priority for lawyers. Many of the lawyers of today may not have been mentored themselves in a deliberate or productive way. You should seek out a lawyer with good mentorship skills and, if you find one, follow him around. You can also have several mentors at once. Sometimes the mentoring relationship is not a formal one, but rather one that occurs through circumstance and opportunity.

In an article published in the *Harvard Business Review*, entitled "The Truth About Mentoring Minorities: Race Matters" (2001), David A. Thomas examines the progression of racial minorities through three large US corporations. He finds that the minority professionals who advance the furthest share one characteristic: a strong network of mentors and corporate sponsors.[1] This finding applies to everybody. If you have a good

---

1   Thomas, David A. "The Truth About Mentoring Minorities: Race Matters" (2001) 79 *Harvard Business Review* 98–112.

mentor, you can go further in your career development. If you have to do it on your own, you can still achieve your goals, but you are way ahead of the game if you have a mentor.

This advice applies even if you are planning on leaving law and is completely transferable to academic, business, and institutional or governmental environments.

What to Look for in a Job

Make a list of what you expect from a job. Identify your goals in one column and write down what you need to do to achieve these goals in a second column. If your goal is to be with your family at dinnertime, you need to figure out what you need to do to achieve this goal. For example, you might consider looking for a part-time position or accepting a job from which you can walk home in ten minutes. You must generate creative options for yourself and write them down. If your goal is to work at the United Nations, mark this down and then, in the next column, write down what you need to do to get there. Do you need to get into politics for a few years? Do you need a PhD? Do you need to work for ten years at one place or do you need to work in ten different places within a period of ten years? Start developing these ideas in writing.

When you embark on an associate job search, remember to look at small practices, regional practices, and specialty practices. There are more than twice as many offices available for associate searches as there are for articling searches because many law offices do not have articling programs. These firms are successful and very interesting, but typically students do not notice them because the names of the firms are not familiar to them from the articling process. If you limit your associate search only to those offices that have articling programs, you may find that the range of your opportunities is narrow. When you embark on your associate job search, do not limit your search to the material in your law school's articling handbook. Instead, use the articling handbook as a starting point for a more in-depth analysis of the profession.

The Lure of Money

This is a cautionary note about money. Of course, we would all love a job with a starting salary of $90,000, but you must understand the expectations of a firm that pays such a figure. A firm intends to profit from your work (unless it is a not-for-profit office). If they pay you $90,000, they will expect a return on your salary through your billable hours. To calculate how many hours you will need to bill in order for a firm to break even on your overhead (support staff, dues and insurance, office rent, IT, etc.), multiply the proposed salary by 2.5 to 3.5 (depending on the city). Then, take this figure and divide it by your likely hourly billing rate as a first-year associate. This sum will generate the minimum number of hours you will need to bill for the firm to break even. For example:

$90,000 (salary) x 3.0 = 270,000 / $150 (hourly rate) = 1800 billable hours

Remember that your billable target and the number of hours you work in the office are not identical. Depending on the type of work you do and what the expectations are for non-billable work, it may be reasonable to multiply the target billable hours figure by a factor of 2.0 in order to calculate how many hours you will need to be in the office so as to meet your annual target. Next, divide this figure by the number of weeks you will be in the office (forty-eight weeks if you plan to take four weeks of vacation). This calculation will generate the average number of hours you will need to be in the office each week in order to meet your billable target. For example:

1800 billable hours x 2.0 = 3600 / 48 (working weeks) = 75 hours per week

Now, run the same calculation for an office offering a $50,000 salary with a more modest operating cost (lower rent district, fewer staff). You can multiply your salary by a factor of 2.5 instead of 3.0. When making this calculation, remember that your hourly billing rate as a first-year associate may go down a bit.

$50,000 (salary) x 2.5 = 125,000 / $125 (hourly rate) = 1000 billable hours

And then,

1000 billable hours x 2.0 = 2000 / 48 (working weeks) = 42 hours per week

Be careful if you find yourself saying, "I will work for a few years at these high-paying law firms, pay off my debt and then do something else." This is a wonderful plan if you can do it, but take care that you do not underestimate the power that money may have to change your value system. Money is a tool which is best used as a means to an end. If you do not handle the money that you are earning carefully, you might end up dependent on it. A dependency on money may narrow the range of your future job options.

You have probably heard this called the *golden handcuffs*. The catchphrase seems trite when you consider the potential consequences of living on a high-paying salary for more than a few years. There is a correlation between choice and happiness in career searches. You should be cautious about introducing factors that will reduce the number of choices you have and your ability to seek out your ideal career. Be very clear about your purpose and goals when considering money issues.

Pursue Your Personal Goals

Remember to pursue your original goals: the goals that brought you to law school and those that you developed while you were in law school. Many students enter law school because they want to change the world and make a difference. With a law education and practical experience, you are now in the best position to achieve these goals. Do not give up on your goals. Many negative comments are made about lawyers; some are warranted, most are not. Try to ignore these comments and continue to pursue your laudable goals.

How to Embark on an Associate Job Search

How do you embark on an associate job search? First, you ought to keep a file on yourself.[2] You should keep the business cards of all the people you meet. When you return home after an event where there has been an exchange of business cards, write where you met each person on the back of his card because you will likely forget this information over time.

Keep a record of all the jobs you have ever applied for, including the job description and the cover letters you sent. You should also keep a record of what you accomplished when you summered, articled, or worked at a legal aid clinic. Take note of publications that you co-authored and publications in which you received special recognition. Track the case law citations of any cases that you assisted on.

Your goal is to develop a plan using a method similar to the one you would use when developing a client file. Be open to suggestions. When others speak to you, let them stimulate your creativity. Learn how others developed their careers and listen to their wise suggestions. The skills that you acquired while articling — your organizational techniques, your time management techniques, your ability to focus on important issues —are skills that you can transfer to a business, academic, or institutional setting.

Plan for Change

Be sure to plan for change. It has become axiomatic to say that change is one of the only constants in life. If you have a goal, factor in the possibility that once you get to where you think you want to be, everything will have changed. Remember that your values, beliefs, and ideals are constantly changing as you encounter different experiences. In order to balance these changes, you ought to incorporate what you plan on doing next in stages. This way, you will be flexible if your goals change or if the market shifts. Those who have a broad plan and malleable targets will be more likely to be satisfied with their achievements than those with narrow, fixed objectives.

Navigate Reasonably Through Reality

I have advised students in the past to *navigate reasonably through reality*.

By *navigate*, I mean operate strategically. This is not a game; however, the navigational tools and strategies that you employ when you are playing strategy games such as chess, golf, or even video games should be applied to your career development.

By *reasonably*, I mean have a reasonable understanding of yourself and your abilities. You should also have a reasonable understanding of the employment environment that you are about to enter. If your goals are reasonable, you should be able to achieve them.

---

2   See the "Sample Organizational System" on page 122.

By *reality*, I mean that your actions should not be based upon other peoples' perceptions of the world, including those that come from television, professors, career services offices, family, and friends. You should pursue your own goals and your own happiness. Follow what you consider to be your reality and pursue it vigorously. You should be able to find a reasonable combination of work and private life. If you do not, change your environment so that it matches your values.

Working productively is one of the most satisfying experiences you will encounter, yet many people speak about their jobs with dread. There is nothing better for your self-esteem than having a great day at work and coming home satisfied, or even exhausted, because you have accomplished your day's goals. Law students are not afraid of hard work; you gained admission into law school and you survived it by working hard. On the other hand, law students are, quite reasonably, afraid of unrealistic work expectations and unsatisfying work experiences.

Capitalize on Haphazard Events

In a job search, it is important to be able to capitalize on haphazard events. You may find that other people tell you that they *fell into* the job or they got the job through their neighbour's cousin. How can you capitalize on haphazard events? The best thing you can do is to try to increase the opportunities for these events to occur. You may be able to increase your exposure by joining your province's bar association and your city's law association (if you are not already a member). You can also increase your exposure by going to alumni functions or other networking events, and attending seminars and conferences in practice areas that interest you. These are some of the ways you can create opportunities for introductions and random job offers.

Change Your Resumé

It is time to update your resumé. You will need to revise the resumé you had when you were a student. You are now entering into a much more professional stage of your career. Remove all references to high school and non-professional summer jobs you had when you were an undergraduate student. Add descriptions of the rotations you are going through in your articles and consider listing some of the exceptional work you are doing while articling. Remember to include your anticipated call to the Bar. Indicate the month, year, and province of your expected call in your education section.

The value placed on your law school grades is slowly going to diminish as you advance as an associate. You should still mention any awards received in university, but do not assume that you will be submitting your grades when you apply for an associate position.

You should also change your references. Select referees from people with whom you articled or opposing counsel from another firm who got to know your work as an articling student. Your professional experience and reputation are becoming more significant than your academic abilities as you advance as an associate. For this reason, some of the reference letters you have from professors may not be as relevant as they were when you were putting together articling applications.

Change the voice-mail message that you use at home so that it matches the professional level you have achieved. You do not want cute messages on your home telephone answering machine if you are giving your home number to potential employers. Also, do not conduct your job search from the office of your current employer, unless your firm has advised you that they cannot hire you back and has offered to let you use their resources. Your job search should be done on your own time and using your own resources.

Researching Associate Positions

I recommend using the *Alberta Reports*, *Ontario Reports*, *BC Law Reports*, and any other weekly professional notice system to research associate positions. Every lawyer in Ontario receives a weekly, unbound copy of the *Ontario Reports*, the first thirty or so pages of which are filled with seminars, announcements, and career opportunities. Read through these pages to generate ideas about new firms or to look at the jobs available for associates. The associate job market is significantly larger and broader than the articling market. You can also check the websites of the Canadian Bar Association, the various law societies of each province, county and municipal law associations, Workopolis.ca and other general job search websites, as well as the headhunters specializing in law (e.g., ZSA, the Affiliates, Marsden Nagata, RainMaker). Finally, many career services offices are expanding to assist new alumni in associate job searches.

Be sure to read through the industry magazines as well. The more information you can acquire about the profession and various specialties, the better off you will be. Information is incredibly valuable in this job search process. The less you know, the more you risk selecting a position that does not suit you.

Learn from the Experiences of Others

Be sure to speak with people who have been through job changes. They will naturally want to help you and you should let them. Do not limit yourself to partners at law firms. Speak with the secretaries and clerks; they have a tremendous amount of experience with other law firms and can offer you some candid suggestions. This is the time to expand your networking group as much as possible and it is important not to pre-judge people based on title or education.

Carry Your Business Card

When you go to events always bring your business card. Giving out your business card is your best method of ensuring that others will keep your name in mind and get in touch with you in the future.

Ask for Assistance

If you are not returning to the firm with which you articled, it is in the firm's best interest to help you find an associate position. It does not bode well for a firm if it does not hire back half of its students and those students have trouble finding jobs. Firms want to be able to tell their new recruits, "do not worry; if we do not hire you back, you will be able to get a job without difficulty." They wish to preserve their own reputation by helping you find a job, but you must ask them for assistance while they still remember the quality of your work.

Sit down and talk to the lawyers you have worked with within a few weeks of learning about hirebacks. Ask them the names of other firms and find out if they are willing to make a couple of phone calls or recommendations on your behalf. If the opening line of your cover letter reads, "Lawyer A recommended that I apply to your firm," you are off to a great start.

Networking

When you are networking, remember that a networking event can turn into an interview. When I embarked on my associate job search, I asked a lawyer I had briefly worked with about using him as a reference. He ran a small boutique practice and was not hiring at the time, but he generously allowed me to use his name as a reference and even gave me some suggestions. Six months later, he called me up because he had an opening. This opportunity was the direct result of my having been professional throughout the networking encounter and the fact that I had provided him with a copy of my application material. In the end, what I thought was a networking exercise turned out to be an interview, a job for seven years, and a professional colleague for life.

Always give a copy of your resumé to those you speak with about networking. The same goes for those people who agree to be your references.

What do you do if an interview is not working out? It may be possible for you to convert the interview into a networking encounter. Consider speaking with the interviewer about other jobs in the market and see whether this person could give you a couple of names. He or she may be willing to introduce you to others.

How to Introduce Yourself

Before you attend a function, decide whether you are there as a delegate representing your office, or you are there for your own experience. When someone says, "Very nice to meet you. What is your name?" do not simply give your name. Add that you are there on behalf of your office, including your title if necessary. Speak clearly and confidently during an introduction; if a person doesn't hear your name or misunderstands who you are, it is very difficult to have a productive conversation with that person.

Introduce Yourself to Everyone

Remember to introduce yourself to everyone you meet, including spouses. Do not make assumptions about people you do not know at a business or social event. Although you may be eager to speak with the managing partner at the firm picnic, be careful not to overlook the fact that his spouse is the vice president and general counsel of a public company. Treat everyone as equally important in a networking environment.

Arrive Early

Another important tip is to arrive at the event early. You are more likely to be remembered if you come early or on time and your promptness will be appreciated by the host. On the other hand, try not to be the last person to leave the function, unless you are personal friends with the host. Be sure to thank the host on your way out; do not simply "disappear."

Name Tags

No one likes to wear name tags, but it is important to wear them if they are offered because they really make a difference. People tend to avoid a person whose name they do not know or cannot remember. Be sure that your name is written clearly so that people can read it and comfortably pronounce your name. For difficult or unusual pronunciations, consider finding a word that rhymes with your name so that you can help the person with whom you are speaking with the proper pronunciation.

Remembering Names

A good way to remember a person's name is to shake his hand upon meeting him, immediately repeating his name when you say you are pleased to meet him. If you say the name a couple of times during the conversation, you are more likely to remember it later. If you simply listen to the name during the introduction, the name is more difficult to remember. Repeating a person's name speaks to the art of active listening. Be sure to pay attention when someone is talking to you and respond to the comments that he makes. Try not to change the topic when he is speaking, especially if he is significantly more senior than you.

Following Up

Send a thank-you note (or e-mail) if it is appropriate or telephone the host to thank him after an event.

Meeting People

Few people enjoy networking events. When most people enter a room and see seventy-five people, they get a bit overwhelmed. To succeed in a networking environment, you only need to have two or three sustained conversations. You do not need to meet everyone; you may undermine your ability to network if you spread yourself too thin. Move through the room purposefully, not aimlessly. For example, as you walk towards the food table, deliberately pass by someone with whom you would like to chat. If she is in another conversation with another person when you reach her, continue towards the food table as you had planned. This tactic will keep you moving and allow you to avoid just standing in a corner somewhere. Also, try to approach a person from the front; do not creep up behind someone and tap her on the shoulder.

Conclusion

The associate job search takes place in stages. It is important to allow the dynamic process of the search to develop over time. As you learn more information and incorporate what you know into your plan, you may find that your career goals shift.

If you are about to finish, or have just finished, articling, you are probably exhausted (understandably so). Articling is a very tiring process. You may feel as if you have just completed a year-long interview. Now you must begin the process of starting your career, another tiring process. You must give yourself time to reevaluate what you think about yourself.

If you have not been invited to return to your firm, you might feel defeated and frustrated. Or, you may have chosen a law firm that did not meet your expectations, and you now realize that your goals have changed. Such an experience has an element of personal defeat in it. You may also experience frustration when attempting to redefine your goals. In a situation like this, you will benefit from performing an analysis of your experiences.

Capturing opportunities involves being open to new experiences and being flexible. The more you know and the more you experience, the more likely you will be to pursue a satisfying career.

The Associate Job Interview

Interviewing for an associate position can be a different experience from that that of interviewing for a summer or articling job. By the time you interview for an associate position, you will have file experience and experience with clients. You are also likely to have a better sense of what you intend to pursue at this stage of your professional career. While the law firms that interviewed you for summer and articling positions sought to understand your goals and your character, law firms interviewing you for associate positions will likely want to know about the experiences that you have had.

You should prepare for the associate interview differently from the way in which you prepared for an articling interview. Prepare by making notes and lists of the files and of the clients you have dealt with. These notes and lists are preparatory and for your purposes only. If you make these notes and lists before you send off your applications, you may be able to incorporate some of the information contained in them into your cover letter or your resumé.

There are five different areas of law practice upon which a good interviewer for an associate position will probably question you:

1. Substantive law
2. Type of legal work
3. Type of clients
4. Business aspects of a law practice
5. Work styles

Each law firm will place emphasis on one of these areas more than another, depending on how the firm operates. If you know lawyers who work at the office, or if you research the firm before you interview, you may be able to make a reasonable estimate as to which area will be focused on during the interview.

1. **Substantive law.** Before your interview, review the different areas of law and legal issues you encountered when you were an articling student. These areas include broad categories such as tax or real estate law,[3] as well as more refined sub-categories such as GST issues and mortgages. If you are interviewing at a boutique firm, or if you are interviewing to be placed within a boutique department in a large law firm, it is important to focus on the more detailed issues you have encountered. Reflect on these issues and what you learned when working on the files and be sure to be accurate about your work experience. Most law firms will assume that you have had only introductory experience during articles, unless you articled at a boutique firm where you spent your entire articles within one area of law (in which case you will have detailed experience within that area).

    During the interview, you may be asked to discuss the work that you did on a file. In most cases, it is appropriate to generally describe the law, the issues that you covered, and the type of work that you did, but be sure not to mention the client's name or too many details about the transaction because this may be a breach of client confidentiality.

2. **Type of legal work.** It is quite common to be asked what type of legal work you have done during an associate interview. This is a broad question designed to allow the firm to better understand which files they can assign to you and what training they will need to give you. Given the volume of files you are likely to have encountered during articles, it is wise to make a separate list of the different types of work you have done. It is important to study this list so that you will be able to recall the information with ease during the interview. Examples of work done for civil litigation practices include motions, hearings, applications, mediations, arbitrations,

---

3   Refer to the "Sample Practice Areas" on page 119 for examples.

pre-trials, trials, appeals, assessments, discoveries, and settlement conferences. Within each of these areas is the preliminary work such as legal research, drafting pleadings, and factum writing. Examples of work done for corporate law include share transfers, asset transfers, debt financing, initial public offerings, due diligence, trust agreements, and escrow agreements. Again, remember the detailed work that you may have done, including drafting clauses, preparing record books, filings, negotiating, and attending closings.

3. **Type of clients.** It is important not to risk client confidentiality when answering questions about the types of clients you have worked for. There are ways to avoid breaching confidentiality. For instance, you can group clients into broad categories such as institutional, government, public companies, banks, family businesses, small corporate clients, individual clients, celebrities, estates, trusts, and beneficiaries. Speaking about clients as a group will preserve confidentiality while allowing you to discuss what you have been exposed to.

4. **Business aspects of a law practice.** Another area that an interviewer will likely cover in an associate job interview is the administrative side of practising law. This includes opening and closing files, billing clients and collecting fees, docketing and trust ledgers, marketing and seeking out new clients, and participating in committee work for the larger practices. Your exposure to the business side of a law practice will depend on the type of firm at which you articled. Larger law firms have accounting departments so if you worked for a large firm you may not have been exposed, aside from docketing, to the financial management of the practice. If you worked for a smaller firm, you may have worked with a file from the initial client meeting to the closing of the file. As a result, you will be able to discuss your experience with administrative tasks in your associate job interview. Those who have worked on small claims court matters may be especially familiar with the procedural side of law.

5. **Work styles.** Every articling student who has worked with more than one lawyer is able to speak about work styles. Some lawyers micromanage the work while others leave juniors with many decisions to make on their own. Some lawyers prepare for matters well in advance while others do most of the work immediately before a deadline. Some lawyers are more organized than others while other lawyers are more patient. Whether you work well with one lawyering style or another depends largely on your own work habits and preferences. The more you understand your own work style, the better you will be able to steer the conversation to your advantage.

The more you prepare in advance to discuss the areas of law outlined above, the more likely it is that you will be able to articulate your ideas effectively during an interview. Make an effort to recall the areas of law to which you have been exposed and all of your experiences in these areas. Your efforts will enable you to communicate what the firm needs to know about your work experience and improve your chances of getting hired for the job.

eight: Practice Management & Organization

Much has been written recently on practice management and it is likely that, at an early stage in your career, your law office will run a seminar or encourage you to attend a professional program on the topic. In order to develop good work habits, it is wise to begin to learn about practice management as soon as possible, whether you are a summer student, an articling student, or an associate. There are three areas of practice management and office organization that it will be beneficial for you to focus on: creating a stress-free (or stress-reduced) work environment; avoiding professional liability; and increasing efficiency. These areas are connected to one another; advice pertaining to one area will often pertain to the other areas as well. It is always a good idea to keep these areas in mind, even when you are a student, so that you will reflect upon your developing work style and observe the habits of the lawyers with whom you work.

The stage you have reached in your law career will likely determine the area upon which you focus most of your attention. For instance, an articling student might focus on reducing stress and pay relatively little attention to professional liability, except to learn why certain systems and routines are adhered to by lawyers. An associate, on the other hand, might be more interested in efficiency. A lawyer once made the following insightful observation: until you have completed a closing, a motion, or any assignment at least once, you will have no idea how to accomplish the task efficiently. An associate, because she will have some file experience, will be able to focus on efficiency. It is a truth universally acknowledged that one of the best methods for reducing stress is to be efficient. A high level of efficiency will enable you to deal with a heavy workload without feeling that you are overburdened.

The most important benefit to be derived from attending seminars or reading advice on practice management, aside from learning some useful tips, is an increased awareness of how you organize your workload, your office, your files, and your day. A good deal of the advice given at seminars, or in books, on practice management is intuitive. Most of the advice must be tailored to suit an individual's specific office environment and work preferences. Slavishly following advice may backfire if you do not make sure that the practice management system you design for yourself is attuned to your specific work habits and the level of responsibility you have in the office.

Reduce Stress

The goal of most office organization systems is to create and maintain a calm and predictable office environment so that people can get their work done. Stress in the workplace is not necessarily connected to the nature of the work done there. For some people, stress in the workplace is connected to an inability to control their environment. Stress might be the result of a person's lack of knowledge as to what they will be working on during the week, over the course of the day, or over the next few hours. This uncertainty creates a sense of helplessness. Significant amounts of stress can reduce cognitive functioning, shorten attention spans, and impair judgment. It is important for you to manage your work and your work environment in a manner that reduces unnecessary stress so as to avoid such problems.

Here are a few recommendations that will help both law students and practising lawyers to create a work environment that is relatively calm:

1. **Make a List at the Start of Your Day.** Every morning, when you enter your office, you should adhere to the same pattern of behaviour. Try not to rush straight into your files in the morning. Instead, spend the first ten minutes of each day making a list of what you intend to accomplish that day. The list will help you to judge how much time you will be able to devote to each file. If unexpected, urgent matters arise regularly in your office, be sure to allot time for them on your list. The list will assist you in prioritizing the tasks you need to complete and help you to establish what needs to be done first. As far as it is possible to do so, stick to the list. It will help

you maintain control over your workday. Eventually the list will take the form of a file list (see the "Sample File List" on page 123).

2. **Make Another List at the End of Your Day.** Every evening, before you leave your office, take ten minutes to make a list of what you expect to accomplish the next day. The list has a double function: it will enable you to organize your work for the next day and it will help you to relax once you leave the office. All too often, lawyers will remember important issues that need to be dealt with the next day while eating dinner, or worse, in the middle of the night. Sudden work-related thoughts that arise during your private time will make it difficult for you to separate work from leisure and prevent you from resting before your next day of work. Taking ten minutes at the end of your workday to plan your work for the next day will reduce, and possibly eliminate, work-related thoughts that encroach on your private time. If your list is reliable, the first ten minutes of the next day can be used to incorporate any urgent matters that arose the night before into your list and to prioritize your tasks. Once you begin to work from file lists, list-making will become an extremely efficient and effective tool for organization.

3. **Use Technology.** If you are at home and suddenly remember a file that will need attention when you reach the office the next day, rather than trying to remember the file through the night, use technology to help you out. Send yourself a message using e-mail or call into your voice mail to remind yourself to deal with the file. When you reach the office the next day, you will receive the message and amend your list of tasks for the day. The advantage to sending a message to yourself at your office is that you do not need to use your memory to recall the file. In order to fully relax when you are at home, you need to avoid thinking about work issues.

4. **Avoid Emotional Spats.** Some lawyers try to lure other counsel into engaging in emotional spats by writing provoking letters. If you are working on a file and opposing counsel is behaving in this way, avoid rising to the bait. A lawyer who writes, "I am shocked by your position," is making the mistake of confusing the position of the lawyer to whom he is writing with that of the lawyer's client. It would have been better if the lawyer had adopted a more professional tone, for example, "I am surprised by the position taken by your client." You must endeavour to articulate your client's case dispassionately. If a lawyer tries to attack you personally, resist the urge to respond. A refusal to engage in bickering of this nature is the best way to condemn a personal attack. Focus on the legal issues and avoid using emotional language in your business letters. No matter how maddening opposing counsel may be, do not communicate your frustration in your correspondence. If you cannot deal with a file reasonably, logically, and dispassionately, you are not serving your client well.

Professional Liability

One of the reasons LawPRO, the insurer for lawyers in Ontario, publishes free information and sends representatives to speak at seminars on practice management is because an organized lawyer is less likely to be a negligent lawyer. Professional negligence involves many things, including missing limitation periods and mismanaging clients' information and instructions.

Professional conduct is not only about avoiding solicitor's negligence claims or misconduct hearings, but also about servicing your client in a manner that satisfies your client's needs. All too often, a client's misgivings about his lawyer centre on the lawyer's failure to keep the client informed in a diligent and timely manner. The following pointers will help you to meet your clients' needs. They will also help you to keep your clients up-to-date with respect to the progress you are making on their files.

1. **Make Note of Limitation Periods.** For files with limitation periods, make sure that you clearly write the limitation period on the front of the file. This practice will alert all those who work on the file of the limitation period. Ideally, this should be done when you are first retained to work on the file, but sometimes issues come up after the file has been opened that give rise to new claims and, therefore, new limitation periods. Also, write the limitation period in your calendar. Include a bring forward reminder for at least a month before the limitation period expires so that you can address the matter properly before the period expires. If you ever leave your practice, either temporarily or permanently, it is essential that you clearly indicate all limitation periods in the transfer memos you leave for the lawyers who will succeed you.

2. **Send out Client Copies.** Your client should have copies of all the documents and correspondence that are in your file, unless she specifically states that she does not want them. Help your client set up a file to store the material you send to her. At the initial client meeting, give the client a set of file folders and indicate that she should put the documents you send her in reverse chronological order. Clients who have not worked with lawyers before will appreciate the coaching and will be better able to follow the file's progress. They will be less likely to become confused and better able to instruct you effectively.

3. **Print Client Labels.** In order to make it easier for you to send your client copies of all of the letters and documents you receive from opposing counsel, print a set of your client's address labels and keep it in the correspondence brad. Also, buy a *copy* stamp. When new letters and documents arrive for the file, photocopy them, stamp them *copy*, and send them to your client in an envelope with one of the pre-printed client address labels affixed to it. This process should take two minutes, rather than the ten minutes required to write a cover letter containing the obvious and unnecessary statement, "please find enclosed copies of material received . . . ." When you send your client copies of letters and documents that require your commentary or recommendations, you may need to send a cover letter.

4. **Do Not Place Client Files on Top of Other Client Files.** Never open up a client's file on top of another client's open file. Also, avoid having more than one client file open at a time on your desk. There is too great a risk of accidentally placing one client's document into another client's file. It is difficult to avoid having two files open at once when you are working on one file and receive a telephone call regarding another file. When this situation arises, find another surface upon which to open the second file (e.g., a credenza or even a chair). When you finish the telephone call, close the second file and return to your original work. To enable yourself to have only one open file on your desk at a time, work from file lists. If you work from file lists, you will have a good sense of your workload and you will not have to store the files in your office and clutter up your surface area.

5. **Keep a Telephone Log.** You should keep a log in which you document all the telephone calls you receive. Keep a careful record of all the telephone calls you have returned so that you are aware of the calls that still require a response (see the "Sample Telephone Log" on page 124). If you work in an office that uses message slips for telephone calls, staple the message slips into the telephone log to avoid misplacing them. It is unprofessional for a lawyer to lose track of her telephone messages. You must develop a system that will ensure that you respond to all of your calls.

6. **Respond Promptly to Calls, E-mails, and Letters.** In an ideal office, telephone calls are returned within twenty-four hours, e-mails are replied to within forty-eight hours, and letters are responded to within one week. If you are working on a trial, a closing, or you are exceptionally busy with other matters, respond to your messages by indicating that you are involved in another matter and will reply to the content of the message in ten days (or however long you expect to be). If you go on vacation or you are ill for a few days, you should indicate that you are absent in your voice-mail message and you should set an auto-reply message for any e-mails you might receive.

Increase Efficiency

Working efficiently does not necessarily mean working quickly. Sometimes, especially when things get very busy, you will need to slow down in order to ensure that you accomplish everything without making errors. You can observe this phenomenon during triage in hospitals; doctors appear to be moving slowly, despite the urgency of the situation. These professionals are trained to follow a specific procedure when determining the order in which patients will receive treatment, usually giving priority to those who are the most severely ill. This practice guarantees that doctors do not skip critical steps in their evaluation and resolution of an urgent situation.

In some ways, law is no different. Lawyers who adopt set routines are often able to develop a reliable system that allows them to deal with their administrative work efficiently and productively. Set routines and habits can calm the mind and better enable lawyers to focus on their work.

1. **Keep a List of Your Active Files.** Rather than piling up files on your credenza, make a list of your active files. Print a revised copy of your list of active files every week and use it as a *to do* list. An active files list will help to increase the amount of surface area available in your office so that you do not have to open files on top of one another. Such a list will also provide you with a detailed record of your workload, making it easier for you to assess what needs to be done. You will find it helpful to review your active file list in the first and last ten minutes of each day. You can also use the file list to highlight any limitation periods that will occur within the month. Finally, keeping active files in a filing cabinet until you need them, rather than on your desk, will prevent you from being interrupted by support staff who need access to the files.

2. **Use Binders.** Most offices have both pads of writing paper and three-ringed binders containing paper for their lawyers to use. Most lawyers opt for the pads of paper; however, it is more practical to use a binder along with a set of two or three dividers. Place your active files list and telephone logs at the front of the binder. Use the rest of the binder to make notes during meetings, to review files, and for legal research. Working with a binder will secure your notes in one place until you are ready to place them in the file. You can allow your notes to accumulate over the week and then take ten minutes out of Friday to file them in their proper files.

3. **Block Periods of Time for Work.** Lawyers tend to block periods of time in their calendars for meetings or court dates only. Rarely do they block off two hours to work privately on a file in their offices. The benefit of working in solitude on one file is that it increases a lawyer's ability to focus on the file and examine it in detail. When working during a period of time that you have blocked off, do not take calls on other files unless they are urgent. Also, discourage your support staff from interrupting your work unless they wish to discuss the file.

4. **Create Administrative Routines.** Once you have worked in an office for about a year, you will have a good sense of when your more productive period occurs. Many people find that they are more productive at certain times in the day (e.g., in the early morning or in the late afternoon). Consider working on difficult tasks during your more productive period, when your ability to concentrate is higher. Work on less difficult, yet necessary, administrative tasks during your less productive period, when your ability to concentrate is lower. For instance, if you find that you are less productive when you return from lunch, use this time to open your mail, respond to e-mails, render accounts, or read through the weekly law reports and professional magazines.

5. **Work on All Files.** Every lawyer has at least one semi-dormant file that gives him a headache. Do not neglect a file because it seems unpleasant. If you do, you may find that complications arise over time. All too often, the only reason the file seems unpleasant to you is because you have put off working on the file for so long that you will have to re-learn the file to get the job done. In order to avoid such situations, make sure that you cycle through your whole file list every six weeks (or whatever period is reasonable, given your file load). Paying regular attention to your files helps to keep them fresh in your memory and increases your efficiency. Also, a wise lawyer will work on the hardest file first and then move on to the easier files. The knowledge that there are other impending files to deal with will keep you focused on the difficult file and help you to get the job done efficiently. The easier files will seem like a reward after you have accomplished the unpleasant task of dealing with the hard file.

6. **Format Your Calendar to Suit Your Needs.** It is important to choose a calendar that is organized in a way that suits your needs. If your office requires you to work with a computer calendar so that others can access your schedule, be sure to format the calendar so that it conforms to your preferences. If you can choose your own calendar system, spend the extra time and money to find one that does what you want it to do.

7. **Keep Your Support Staff Informed.** Keep your support staff, especially law clerks, up-to-date with respect to the content of the files with which they are assisting you. Elicit their thoughts and ideas on matters. Remember, your support staff may spend as much time on the file as you do. They may be able to raise issues or spot problems that you might otherwise overlook, especially if they understand how the file is progressing.

Practice management and office organization require you to decide what works best for you in your work environment. Remember to focus on the three goals of reducing stress, avoiding professional liability, and increasing efficiency. Those who are new to working in a law office, and those who find that they cannot get on top of their workload, may find that advice on these matters can be very helpful, provided that they adapt the advice to suit their preferences.

nine: **Samples**

The following samples are provided to assist students and new lawyers in the preparation of their resumés and cover letters, to help them develop well-constructed responses to frequently-asked job interview questions, to provide them with guidance when they are choosing their career paths, and to help them organize their work once they have jobs.

Sample Resumé and Analysis

The sample resumé and cover letter are each followed by an in-depth analysis that explains, on a line-by-line basis, what should be included in an effective job application. Note that the numbered lines on the sample resumé correspond to the numbered entries in the resumé analysis and that the numbered lines on the sample cover letter correspond to the numbered entries in the cover letter analysis. The sample resumé and cover letter need not be followed to the letter; you should adjust them to suit your individual situation and goals.

Sample Resumé

Perfect Student   *1*

7 Rental Avenue, City, Postal Code
(789) 123-4567   *2*
perfectstudent@lawschool.ca   *3*

Education	200x–(200x)	**Full Name of Law School** *4*
		Bachelor of Laws Candidate *5*

	200x	Admitted to Business Program *6*
	200x	Duty Counsel — Legal Aid Name *7*
	200x	Junior Editor of Law Journal
	200x	ABC Entrance Scholarship *8*

	200x	**Canadian Securities Certificate** *9*

	200x–200x	**Full Name of University**
		Honours Bachelor of Arts *10*
		Major in Economics with a Minor in Asian Studies *11*

	200x	Athletic Award and Faculty Scholar
	199x	University Entrance Scholarship (Renewable)

Work Experience	Summer 200x	**YMCA, City** *12*
		Computer Camp Counselor *13*
		Computer day camp for low-income families *14*
		Responsible for 25 campers *15*

	Summer 200x	**Bank of Montreal, City**
		Bank Teller
		Responsible for over $25,000 daily in transactions *16*
		Bilingual branch (English and Urdu) *17*
		Continuing part-time during law school (200x–200x) *18*

	Summer 200x	**Remax Realtron, City**
		Reception and Webposting Clerk
		Responsible for daily MLS postings
		Responsible for customer service *19*

Work Experience, cont'd.

200x   **Indian Banking Association, Bangalore**
Call Centre Trainer (12-month contract) *21*

Responsible customer service training *22*
Bilingual Trainer in English and Urdu
Average of 45 trainees per class
Awarded employee of the month on three occasions *23*

Summer   **The Gap, City**
200x–200x   Greeter (200x), Sales Associate (200x–200x) *24*

Summer 200x   **Undergraduate University Economics Department, City**
Research Assistant *25*

R.A. for Professor Marcel Sanjay on the effect of markets
in South and North Asia

200x–200x   **Rental Office, University Name**
Filing Clerk and Intake Information Officer

Part-time position *26*

School and Community Involvement *27*

200x–200x   Law School Name Variety Show
200x–200x   Law School Name Touch Football League
200x–200x   Club Member: South Asian Students, Business
         Association *28*
200x–200x   University Varsity Soccer League (Forward)
200x–200x   Out of the Cold Food Bank, City

Other Interests

Languages: fluent in Urdu, conversational in German *29*
Sports: soccer, beach volleyball, hiking, rock climbing *30*
Travel: India, Germany *31*
Music interests: jazz (Coltrane, Mingus) *32*
Music experience: piano (Royal Conservatory, grade 8) *33*
Reading: detective and mystery novels *34*

Resumé Analysis

Pay attention to the white space around your text. This space is important for visual clarity and allows room for the interviewer to make notes on your resume. Use white or off-white paper. Ensure that your tabs and margins are consistent and even. Choose a font that is easy to read. It is preferable to use the same font and size throughout. Separate your personal information from the content of your resumé using a streamlined visual effect (avoid ornate tildes, etc.). Boldface type gives a more streamlined effect than underlining because underlining tends to clutter the white space. Use italics only if necessary.

Please note that the numbered entries below correspond to the numbered lines on the preceding sample resumé.

Personal Information

1. Place your name in boldface type so that it stands out clearly and distinctly at the top of your resumé. If you have a gender-neutral name, consider adding Ms. or Mr. Match the header of your resumé with the header of your cover letter so that they are easily identifiable as a set.

2. Place just one telephone number on your resumé, preferably a number that is active from the day you submit your application through to your call day. Ensure that your voice-mail message is professional and clear.

3. Use a professional e-mail address. Use the address your law school gives you in order to emphasize the school you are attending. Do not include a website if it is a personal site. You should only include a website if it is a part of your professional portfolio (e.g., if you were once a web designer).

Education

4. Include the full, formal name of your law school. Work in reverse chronology.

5. Remember that you are a Bachelor of Laws *candidate*. Use the LLB (or JD) initials if you wish, but keep the name of the degree consistent with the name of your undergraduate degree (initials for all degrees or full name for all degrees). Mark the anticipated year of graduation in brackets because it has not yet occurred.

6. If you have been admitted to an intensive program or an exchange program that has not yet begun, mark the year in brackets. You will be able to speak about what you expect to gain from the program during your interview.

7. You may include your academic-related work in the education section. This will allow you to separate your extra-curricular academic work (e.g., legal aid) from your non-academic employment (e.g., pub management). Alternatively, you may wish to

have a separate section for your law school involvement. Be wary of having too many sections; they may disrupt the chronology and confuse your interviewer.

8. You may include scholarships and awards in the education section. If you do so, when the interviewer is reviewing your education, she will immediately see that you are an above-average student. Do not include the value of the scholarship. List any bursaries that had an achievement component in addition to a financial need component. Work in reverse chronology for all awards.

9. Place all professional certificates and diplomas in the education section.

10. Remember to include the name of your undergraduate degree (BA, BSc, BComm etc). If you do not have a full undergraduate degree, indicate this clearly (e.g., two years towards a Bachelor of Arts). Be sure to indicate the start and end dates for each academic program by year (the month is not necessary and will clutter the page).

11. Include your areas of study.

Work Experience

12. Place the name of your employer and the city in which you worked in boldface type. Province names are unnecessary. Indicate the time period you worked for the employer in a few words (e.g., summer, winter). It is not necessary to indicate the months. Work in reverse chronology.

13. Mark your job title clearly or summarize your responsibilities in the form of a title.

14. Be sure include a brief description of the job or the employer if it is not obvious what your job entailed. Use as few adjectives as possible.

15. Use words suggesting responsibility and management skills if possible.

16. Include work responsibilities that demonstrate high skill levels and trustworthiness.

17. Include multilingual employment if possible. This is a tremendous asset.

18. If summer employment continues into the school year as a part-time job, include it in the summer description. Try not to divide one employer into two sections.

19. Include customer service experience. Remember, law is a service-oriented profession.

20. Indicate your name on the second page in case the page gets separated from the first page.

21. If a job is contractual, indicate that this is the case in the line containing the job title so that it is not assumed you quit or were fired.

22. For important jobs, include more lines of description. The extra lines will visually indicate that it was a significant work experience for you.

23. Include employee awards.

24. Do not overstate the level of responsibility you had in your lower-level jobs. If you do, it will divert the interviewer away from your more significant work experience. If you received a promotion, indicate the progress you made in your job title or in the description of the job.

25. If you held the position of a research assistant, remember to include the name of the professor you worked for and the area of research. Be prepared to answer questions about the research during your interview. If possible, re-read the article that you helped the professor research before your interview.

26. Include all the work experience you gained during your university education. Omit high school work experience, unless it was exceptional and it is directly related to your area of interest in law.

School and Community Involvement

27. It is not necessary to separate school involvement from community involvement. List your involvement either in reverse chronology or based on involvement (most to least involved).

28. Be accurate about your participation in law school clubs. Include all clubs of which you are a member. These clubs will provide good material for small talk at the beginning of your interview.

Other Interests

29. Include all the languages in which you are conversant. The ability to speak other languages is an extremely marketable asset, especially for a law firm with offices in other countries or a firm that services specific communities. Indicate all of the languages you know with complete accuracy. Expect your interviewer to test your language skills briefly during the interview.

30. Include your athletic involvement. Participation in sports demonstrates teamwork and discipline. Also include non-competitive athletics. Athletic involvement provides a good topic for small talk.

31. Include travel if you have the space. Only list the travel that you have done as an adult, either alone or with friends. Leave out travel that you did with your family as a child, but you may discuss it (if relevant) during an interview.

32. Include a detailed description of your musical interests if you have the space. It will provide you with a targeted topic of conversation during the interview. Be sure to listen to your listed musical interests before the interview.

33. Include your musical achievements. These achievements demonstrate discipline. Be accurate about your formal training.

34. Include your reading interests in as much detail as the space will allow. The interviewer may choose to open the conversation with a discussion of your reading interests. "What are you reading now?" is a common interview question. Be sure that you have recently read books in the areas that you list.

Make sure that your resumé is only two pages long. You may make it three pages long if you have published extensively or if you are a lawyer from another jurisdiction with significant work experience. Do not include references or listings of courses on your resumé. These can appear on separate pages but, in most cases, they are unnecessary.

Sample Cover Letter and Analysis

Sample Cover Letter

Perfect Student   *1*

7 Rental Avenue, City, Postal Code

(789) 123-4567

perfectstudent@lawschool.ca

Date   *2*

First and Last Name of Recruiter   *3*

Director of Recruitment   *4*

Full Law Firm Name   *5*

Street Address, Suite Number, and P.O. Box

City, Province, Postal Code

Dear Ms [Last Name]:   *6*

Re: Summer Student 200x   *7*

Please accept my application for a summer position at [short law firm name]. I am particularly interested in working in your international securities department.   *8*

I have BA in economics with a minor in Asian studies. I have developed these interests by focusing on corporate law (business program for fall 200x) and international conflicts of law (winter 200x). I have also sought out employment to enhance my interests, particularly as an economics R.A. for Professor Marcel Sanjay and with the Indian Banking Association.   *9*

My R.A. work on emerging markets led to a twelve-month contract with the Indian Banking Association (IBA) in Bangalore, India. In my position as a call centre trainer, I was able to merge my bilingual abilities with my understanding of the internationalization of business. I received the employee of the month award three times. While in India, I traveled across the country and visited small start up businesses in Bombay.   *10*

My affiliation with IBA led to my most recent summer position as a bilingual bank teller with the Bank of Montreal. I will continue this position part-time during second-year law school.   *11*

I have researched your firm and I am particularly intrigued by the practice of Gibson Hill who has lectured and published on the globalization of securities markets. I have read Mr. Hill's most recent article in the *Law Times* (June 200x) and would be most interested in being mentored by him and his department.   *12*

I am accustomed to working long hours and remaining with a project until completion. I developed endurance and discipline when I was a Royal Conservatory piano student as a child, and more recently as varsity soccer player. I am confident in my legal research skills and I have been complimented several times on my work as a junior editor of a law journal. I am currently editing a paper on initial public offerings in China.   *13*

Thank you for reviewing my application. I look forward to meeting you.   *14*

Yours sincerely,

Perfect Student   *15*

Encl. (resumé and transcripts)   *16*

Cover Letter Analysis

The purpose of your cover letter is threefold. It functions as (i) a writing sample, (ii) something which highlights certain points on your resumé, and (iii) a means of communicating your area of interest, your reasons for applying to the firm, and your professional work ethic. A cover letter should not exceed one page and a person should be able to read it in about three minutes. You need to develop a tight narrative, use relatively simple sentences, write using the active voice, and avoid hyperbole and overstating your attributes. You should also cross-check your paragraphs to ensure that you have not repeated content or used an unusual adjective more than once.

Please note that the numbered entries below correspond to the numbered lines on the preceding sample cover letter.

1. Match your cover letter header to your resumé header. They form a set.

2. Include the date (this will be the date you sign the letter).

3. Include the first and last name of the recruitment director in the formal address. Be sure to include the formal address, even if you are using a resumé collection process through your law school.

4. Include the formal title of the director.

5. Include the full, formal name of the law firm. LLP stands for limited liability partnership and is part of the formal name of the firm. You need to include LLP in this area only.

6. In the salutation, indicate the gender title and the last name of the recruiter only. Do not include first names in this area.

7. Be sure to include a "re" line that clearly indicates the position for which you are applying. The recruiters receive articling and associate applications at the same time as they receive summer applications.

8. Indicate the area of practice that interests you in the opening paragraph. Keep this paragraph short. If you have two areas of interest, list them. If you do not have a specific area of interest yet, comment on the attractiveness of the rotation system and how it allows you to gain exposure to different areas of the law. Be prepared, however, to narrow your interests during the interview because most law firms place summer students in only one or two departments for the whole summer.

9. Describe your academic history before your work experience, unless you had a career before entering law school. If this is the case, you may be able to market yourself more effectively if you outline your previous career first.

10. Highlight your work experience using groupings that emphasize your strengths. Follow the natural chronology of your experience rather than the reverse chronolo-

gy used in your resumé. Only include necessary information. Draw attention to the areas of your resumé that you would like the recruiter to focus on. Note that the paragraphs describing your academic history, work experience and interest in the law firm should be placed in an order tailored to suit your personal situation.

11. Discuss your most recent work experience in one or two sentences.

12. Include a separate paragraph describing why you are interested in the law firm. This paragraph should be different for each application and should be based on the detailed research you have conducted. Comments on the firm's atmosphere or references to information that can be found on firm's website are weaker than comments about the firm's lawyers or clients.

13. Include a paragraph on your work ethic and use your resumé to develop evidence of your professional character. Relate your work ethic to your extra-curricular activities, your volunteer work, or your other interests. Be sure to provide evidence of your work ethic rather than simply stating that you have one.

14. Your closing paragraph should be brief and not overly ingratiating. There is no need to repeat information contained in your header (such as a telephone number or email address). If you are writing the letter in August and you will have a temporary telephone number until school begins, you may indicate the temporary contact number in your closing paragraph. For example, "For the duration of the summer, until school begins, I may be reached in Vancouver at xxx-xxxx."

15. Remember to sign your letter.

16. "Encl." stands for enclosed. You may list the enclosures if there are only one or two. If you have more than three enclosures, then simply write "Encl."

Sample Cover Letter Sentences

Do not copy these sentences verbatim. Many law firm recruiters will have a copy of this book and those who do will recognize the sentences if you duplicate them. These sentences are designed to provide you with examples of business writing. Take note of how the sentences are front-end loaded with information, use the active voice, and include no more than two adjectives per noun.

1. I am a second-year student at X and would like to apply as a summer student at X.

2. Please accept this application for a summer student position.

3. In response to your web posting, I am applying to your articling student program.

4. I enclose my application for an articling position at X.

5. X, my tax professor, recommended that I apply to your firm for a summer position.

6. I am a second-year law student at X and I am seeking a summer job in the area of X law.

7. I am interested in both X and X law and would be eager to work in either department this summer.

8. I have a general interest in litigation and I am attracted to your firm because of the rotation options in business litigation and health law litigation.

9. I am interested in splitting my summer between working at your firm and working through a fellowship at the Centre for X.

10. I have extensive exposure to securities regulation and I am seeking a summer position connected to securities law.

11. I learned about your firm when I read the article in X magazine about the X trial. I would be very interested in working on this ongoing case.

12. I have been advised by Professor X that your partner, X, is a leader in family law.

13. I am attracted to boutique practices and specialty firms. Before law school, I ran a small business for five years.

14. My interest in litigation began in high school, when I won a debating competition, and continued to grow through law school. My undergraduate minor in theatre has greatly assisted my oratory skills.

15. I developed an interest in defamation law during my previous career in journalism.

16. My work as a telemarketer introduced me to the importance of privacy law.

17. I became interested in patents through my engineering studies.

18. I first learned about education law when I obtained my teachers' certificate.

19. I recently read that X at your firm received an award for X and I am impressed by her dedication to these issues.

20. I am impressed with the quality and volume of cases that your firm handles, including the recent *X v. X* case that has received wide publicity.

21. I am friends with X of your firm and admire her practice. She has spoken highly of her firm and has encouraged me to apply for a summer position.

22. My interest in X law stems from my experience volunteering at X organization.

23. I have been employed by your client X for the past three summers and I have heard many positive things said about your firm.

24. Your website indicates that your firm is a specialist in X area. This is the main reason I have applied to your firm.

25. I have spoken with former summer and articling students of your firm, all of whom speak very highly about the firm, specifically the litigation department.

26. My interest in your firm is because of your strong reputation in X.

27. I first heard about your firm when I attended the Canadian Bar Association X program and listened to X speak.

28. Your commitment to X impresses me. I have shared this commitment for the past decade throughout my work (studies) at X.

29. I was affiliated with your sister firm X in Italy through the X case.

30. I appreciate how forthright your firm is about its exclusivity in the X area of law. I share this focus, which I developed when I studied X in my undergraduate degree.

31. I developed my client/customer service expertise while working as a waiter and sales clerk. These jobs taught me the importance of listening to the consumer.

32. My manager at X frequently praised me for my X and X (creativity, versatility, dedication, promptness, trustworthiness).

33. At X, meeting strict deadlines and working late on projects was a requirement of the job.

34. I am accustomed to independent learning and short turn-around times as a result of working at X.

35. My previous managers have described me as X, X, and X (hard working, accurate, independent, focused, reliable, efficient).

36. My volunteer work with X provided me with X training and access to X processes.

37. My R.A. professor (or duty counsel advisor) trusted me with X research.

38. I have received feedback from my X indicating that I am a X (thorough, creative) thinker (researcher, writer).

39. I taught myself X and I have applied the skills that I have acquired to both my work at X and to my academic studies at X.

40. At X, I was able to demonstrate my abilities in X.

41. During my work at X, I learned the importance of X and X.

42. As a result of my experience traveling abroad, I developed X (independence, cultural sensitivity, new language skills).

43. During my internships at X, I gained valuable experience in X.

44. Given my interest in X, I sought out positions in the X field.

45. I have been trained in X and I have been able to use this skill during my work at X.

46. The nature of the environment/assignments at X required/enabled me to use/apply/integrate my expertise/skills in X.

47. I have worked in professional offices for the past X years and I am accustomed to delivering top-end client service.

48. At X, I was able to demonstrate my abilities in X and learn new skills in X.

49. During my year off between undergraduate studies and law school, I taught myself X and experienced X.

50. Although I grew up in X, I intend to build my career in Toronto.

51. I have lived in X countries and have worked in X different cities. These experiences have taught/enabled me to learn the importance of X and X.

52. I speak X languages proficiently. English is my third language, which I have spoken since age of X.

53. I am drawn to constitutional law because of my family's exposure to X while we lived under the X regime in X.

54. I was raised in an environment where access to justice was rare. My experiences led me to study law and continue to reinforce my commitment to X law.

55. I entered law school because of my involvement in the widely publicized X case.

56. I learned the importance of X from my training in X (piano, skating, baseball, karate) when I was a child.

57. I anticipate that my involvement in X next semester will provide me with X and X opportunities.

58. I look forward to hearing from you.

59. Please do not hesitate to contact me if you have any questions or require further information.

60. Thank you for reviewing my application.

61. Thank you in advance for your consideration.

62. I am eager to hear from you.

63. I am available by e-mail or telephone should you need to reach me.

64. I will be at my parents' home in X until September and can be reached at X should you need to contact me before school begins.

65. I am hopeful that you will grant me an interview so that I may discuss my qualifications in more detail.

66. I look forward to answering your questions during the interview.

67. I am eager to meet you at OCIs.

Sample Interview Questions

The following are sample questions that were asked of students and questions that firms have told me that they like to ask. There are also some questions listed that are rarely asked but, in my opinion, should be discussed during an interview. Space has been left between each question so that you can make notes to help you design an answer.

1. Why did you choose to go to law school?

2. What would you have done if you did not go to law school?

3. What is your favourite course and why?

4. Why did you pick X as a law school?

5. Tell me about your undergraduate lab report (thesis, independent project). [Author's note: Answer this question in less than two minutes. Wait for follow-up questions before elaborating on details.]

6. Why did you choose to apply to this firm?

7. Why did you choose to work in this city?

8. What work experience do you have that you feel is relevant to this position?

9. What do you know about our firm?

10. What are your concerns about working here?

11. Who else are you interviewing with?

12. What did you learn in X course that you feel will be relevant to this job?

13. Are you able to work late nights and on weekends?

14. Describe a situation where you demonstrated client confidentiality.

15. Describe a situation in which you were criticized for your work performance. What did you do to improve?

16. Have you ever been let go from a job? What happened?

17. Describe a situation in which you and your boss/manager did not agree or did not get along. How did you handle it?

18. How did you develop you personal interests?

19. Why do you play X sport? What do you get out of it?

20. Have you studied X law yet? Would you be willing to take this course next term?

21. Why are you going on this exchange? Why did you pick that country/city to study in?

22. How do you feel about representing a client that you know has done something wrong?

23. How would you approach a client who lies to you?

24. What would you do if two important partners want you to work on two big projects at the same time? How would you manage your time?

25. What would you do if you were asked to research a topic of law, but could not find the information?

26. How would you deal with a conflict between articling students?

27. Describe a situation in which you had to get something done but you were not feeling well. What do you generally do in those situations?

28. What would you do if you thought your boss was wrong about an area of the law?

29. What would you do if you found a case that contradicts your argument after you had been to court?

30. Has a client or customer ever been disappointed in your work? What did you do?

31. What is the most important experience you have had so far in law school?

32. What area of the law do you want to practise and why?

33. How many years do you plan on practising law?

34. Do you see yourself more as a team worker or as an independent worker?

35. How would your friends describe your work habits?

36. What have you learned from your parents about work ethics?

37. Who are the role models in your life? Why?

38. How did you learn about our firm?

39. If our firm were to merge with another firm, what would be your two major concerns?

40. Would you be prepared to travel for several weeks at a time for the purposes of work?

41. Describe your study habits.

42. Do you have any questions for us?
    [Author's note: Be sure to have at least one question.]

43. Can you come and visit us again?

44. If you could meet someone else at the firm, whom would you like to meet?

45. If you had to pick a department to work in, what would it be? Why?

46. You do not appear to have any work experience in X area. How do you think this will affect your work performance?

47. Do you prefer working on salary, commission, or a combination of the two? Why?

48. Have you ever worked with someone you did not like? How did you deal with the situation?

49. Explain why you volunteer at X.

50. Explain how you got X job.

51. What did you do at the X company?

52. Why did you leave X job?

53. Why did you take a year off during X? What did you gain from the experience?

54. Why did you switch schools?

55. Why should we hire you over your closest friend?

56. Why do you think you received a grade of C in X course? What did you do after you received the grade?

57. Why do you think you received a grade of A in X course?

58. Describe a situation in which you feel you underperformed. What happened and what did you learn from the experience?

59. Describe a situation in which you felt you were awarded praise when someone else deserved it. What did you do?

60. Have you managed others? What did you learn from the experience?

61. What would you tell the manager at this firm so that she could better manage you?

62. Have you ever lost data or computer files? What happened and what did you do? What do you do to avoid it now?

63. Have you ever made a joke that accidentally offended someone? What did you do about it?

64. Have you ever had to apologize to someone when you felt that you did not need to? How did you approach the situation?

65. Describe a situation in which you failed at something. How did you deal with it?

66. Describe how you would approach a client to tell him that you lost his case in court but you still have to bill him for the work done.

67. Do you have any experience in collecting on accounts receivable? Describe how you might approach someone who is reluctant to pay an account.

68. Have you ever worked in an environment where you docketed your time? Describe what you learned from the experience.

69. What do you think law school has not taught you that will be important to practising law? How do you intend to learn these skills?

70. Are you enjoying interview week? What is the least favourite aspect of this week for you?

71. Are you free for dinner? We would like to introduce you to the head of the hiring committee. [Author's note: If you want the job, the answer is yes.]

72. If we cannot take you on as a summer student, will you still apply for our articling program when we hire twice as many students? [Author's note: Again, if you like the firm, the answer is yes].

Sample Practice Areas

There is a difference between the way the law is divided up for academic purposes and the way it is divided up in practice areas. For instance, there are no "tort" or "contracts" law departments. At the bottom of this list is an area to add to any additional practice areas that you learn about.

1. Aboriginal (also Native)
2. Administrative (also regulatory and judicial review)
3. Advertising
4. Agency
5. Alternative Dispute Resolution
6. Animal Rights
7. Appellate Advocacy
8. Aviation (also transportation)
9. Banking
10. Bankruptcy (also insolvency)
11. Bioscience
12. Capacity Board
13. Child Protection
14. Civil Liberties
15. Class Actions
16. Collections (also debtor/creditor)
17. Commercial
18. Commercial Fraud (also white collar criminal)
19. Communications
20. Community Service
21. Competition
22. Computer
23. Condominium
24. Conflicts of Law (public and private)
25. Constitutional
26. Construction (also engineering)
27. Copyright (also intellectual property)
28. Corporate
29. Corporate Restructuring (also insolvency)
30. Criminal
31. Cross Border
32. Debtor/Creditor
33. Defamation (also libel and slander)
34. Discrimination and Harassment
35. Education
36. E-commerce
37. Employment
38. Entertainment
39. Energy
40. Engineering (also construction)
41. Environmental
42. Estates (also wills)
43. Family
44. Fiduciaries
45. Fisheries
46. Food and Drug
47. Forestry
48. Franchise
49. Freedom of Information
50. Gaming
51. General Practice
52. Global Business
53. Government Regulation
54. Government Offices (all areas of federal, provincial, municipal services)
55. Guardianship (also mental incompetency)
56. Health (also medical)
57. Hotel and Hospitality
58. Human Rights
59. Immigration (also refugee)
60. Industrial
61. Information Technology
62. Initial Public Offerings (also securities)
63. Insolvency (also bankruptcy)
64. Insurance

65. Intellectual Property (also trademarks, patents, and copyright)
66. International Trade and Business
67. Internet
68. Judicial Review (also administrative)
69. Juvenile Detention
70. Knowledge Management
71. Labour (also union)
72. Land Development (also municipal)
73. Landlord and Tenant
74. Leasing
75. Libel and Slander (also defamation)
76. Licensing
77. Maritime
78. Mediation (also ADR)
79. Medical Malpractice
80. Mental Incompetency (also guardianship)
81. Mergers and Acquisitions
82. Military
83. Minority Rights
84. Mining
85. Motor Vehicle
86. Municipal (also land development)
87. Native (also Aboriginal)
88. Natural Resources
89. Negligence
90. Oil and Gas (also energy)
91. Patents (also intellectual property)
92. Personal Injury
93. Pensions
94. Poverty
95. Privacy
96. Privatization
97. Pro Bono
98. Product Liability
99. Professional Discipline
100. Professional Negligence
101. Public Health
102. Public Policy
103. Quasi Criminal and Provincial Offences
104. Real Estate
105. Refugee (also immigration)
106. Regulatory (also administrative)
107. Research
108. Restitution and Remedies
109. Securities
110. Shipping (also transportation)
111. Small Claims
112. Strategic Counsel
113. Sports
114. Tax
115. Technology
116. Test Case Litigation
117. Trademarks (also intellectual property)
118. Transportation (also aviation and shipping)
119. Treaties and Trade
120. Trusts
121. Union (also labour)
122. Waste Management
123. White Collar Criminal (also commercial fraud)
124. Wills (also estates)
125. Workplace Safety
126. Young Offenders
127. _____
128. _____
129. _____
130. _____
131. _____
132. _____
133. _____
134. _____
135. _____

Sample Law Office Structures and Traditional Law Careers

This is a list of the various types of law offices and traditional uses of a law degree. The list is not comprehensive as there are always new and emerging ways to develop a law office. Speak with your career services office for other ideas if you have a preference for setting up or working in an office that is not listed here.

1. Academic
2. Arbitrator
3. Association of lawyers (e.g., sole practitioners in a rent-sharing agreement)
4. Caseworker
5. Clerk (to a judge)
6. Crown Attorney — civil
7. Crown Attorney — criminal
8. Contract lawyer (e.g., to cover a maternity leave, to assist on a specific case)
9. Government lawyer (e.g., federal, provincial, municipal, regional)
10. In-house counsel (e.g., for a corporation or an institution)
11. Internet practice (e.g., on-line advice)
12. Judge
13. Judges' Advocate General (military)
14. Justice of the Peace
15. Legal aid office
16. Master of the court (depending on jurisdiction)
17. Mediator
18. NGO lawyer
19. Private practice — full service
20. Private practice — boutique area of law
21. Private practice — sole practice
22. Pro bono practice
23. Special counsel
24. Tribunal member or hearing panel member

Sample Organizational System

Being organized when you work in a law practice is essential. You must keep track of limitation periods, deadlines, client documents, and client information. Many solicitor's negligence claims arise as a result of a solicitor's failure to remain organized and on top of the information relevant to a file. The earlier you develop reliable organizational systems in your career, the better off you will be. Developing these systems for your job search is good practice for when you are a lawyer.

The more organized you are in your job search, the less likely you will be to miss a deadline or overlook a job posting. Although the following list of files may appear to be overly subdivided, these subdivisions will make it easier for you to locate a document in your files on short notice (e.g., a writing sample, a reference letter). Keep all of your notes and all of the business cards that you collect in the appropriate sub-files until you are called to the Bar. This information will be valuable to you for several years.

These files and folders can be kept on your computer or in hard-copy form (transcripts and reference letters will probably be stored in hard-copy form only). If you store both, it is recommended that you set up your computer and hard copy files so that they are identical to one other.

Sample Main Folder: Second-Year Summer Job Search

General Sub-Files:

> Master Cover Letter and Resumé
> Transcripts and Diplomas
> Reference Letters and Networking Contacts
> Law Society Regulations and Handbooks (for each province)
> Notes on Career Ideas including Personal Workbook

Detailed Sub-Files on Cities:

> Research on Positions in Ottawa
> Research on Positions in Vancouver
> etc.

Detailed Sub-Files on Practice Areas:

> Research on Practising Health and on Firms Practising Health
> Research on Practising Securities and on Firms Practising Securities
> etc.

Detailed Sub-Files on Firms:

> Research on and application to Torys
> Research on and application to Davis & Company
> etc.

Sample File List

A, B & C Law Firm

Organized Lawyer

Week of _____

Files

1. Abbott _____
2. Banjoy _____
3. Caruso _____
4. Bowman _____
5. Farrah _____
6. Gallaway _____
7. Eliah _____
8. Hankel _____
9. Ing _____
10. Olson _____
11. Tasmanian _____
12. Jong _____
13. Kwibecki _____
14. Qatan _____
15. Smith _____
16. Patel _____
17. Lo _____

Administrative

1. Law Society _____
2. Journal Reading _____
3. Billings _____
4. Close Files _____
5. Committee Work _____
6. Other _____
   Other _____

Sample Telephone Log

A, B & C Law Firm

Organized Lawyer

Date	Message	Done
October 21/0X	J. Bonman, re: X — (333) 444-5555	October 22

ten: Personal Workbook

This workbook is designed to allow you to organize your personal thoughts and make notes about your career plans in an orderly fashion. These pages may be expanded and altered according to your individual career path. Filling out this workbook before you meet with the director of career services at your law school may help to give your meetings more focus. Recording information in this workbook will also assist you when you draft your resumé and cover letter and it will also ensure that you do not omit any significant information.

Most students find that their career plan grows and changes when they commence their research and apply for jobs. This workbook will allow you to observe how your thoughts and preferences develop as you move from a summer job search, to an articling job search, to an associate job search. If you begin a career in an area of the law that you later find unsatisfactory, returning to the notes in this workbook may help you to recall other branches of law with which you have had experience.

Personal Background

List your academic focus and preferences in high school.

List your extra-curricular, volunteer, and employment experience in high school.

List the careers that you wanted to pursue when you were in elementary school and in high school.

List your primary and secondary academic focuses during your undergraduate studies.

List your extra-curricular experience, volunteer work, and other involvement during your undergraduate studies.

List your academic focus in your graduate studies (if applicable).

List your work experience during and after your undergraduate studies, including full-time career pursuits.

List any job you had outside of law school, while you were attending law school (e.g., summer jobs, part-time jobs).

List the extra-curricular, student government, mooting, and volunteer work you are doing within law school.

List the careers that your friends, neighbours, and family members have pursued and mark with an asterisk (*) the careers that interest you.

List the languages that you speak.

List the cities that you have lived in or visited and mark with an asterisk the cities you would be interested in working in.

List the hobbies that you have now or had earlier in your life, including athletic activities.

General Areas of Interest

List the reasons why you chose to go to law school. Once you have made the list, rank the reasons with numbers (1 being most significant, 2 being next most significant etc.).

List the career path(s) you would have pursued if you had not gone to law school.

List the areas of law that you anticipated you would be interested in prior to starting law school.

List your favourite law school courses so far.

Emerging Areas of Interest

Review the lists you have generated in the Personal Background and General Areas of Interest sections. Below, make a second list of themes and trends you observe in these lists.

List all the areas of law that currently interest you. Refer to the list of Sample Practice Areas to assist you in generating this list. Once you have made the list, rank the areas by preference (1 being most preferred, 2 being next most preferred etc.).

List collateral areas of law that are related to the areas of interest you listed above. Use the list of Sample Practice Areas to generate this collateral list. For instance, if you are interested in real estate, collateral areas include municipal law, construction liens, etc. If you are interested in civil litigation, make a note of the specific area of law that you would be interested in litigating (e.g., estate litigation, tax litigation, medical malpractice litigation).

List the areas of law from the list of Sample Practice Areas that intrigue you, but you do not know much about at this stage. Ask your career services office about how you can research these areas.

List cases or areas of law that your professors discussed in class that seem interesting to you.

List the areas of law that you learned about from career services seminars, career fairs, law school programs, and law publications (e.g., newspapers, magazines, journals) that interest you.

List current events that you find intriguing and make a note of the areas of law that relate to these events.

List the areas of law that do not interest you. Mark beside each area a short explanation as to why the area does not interest you.

Advanced Areas of Interest

List the areas of law covered in any mooting, memos, facta, or essays you wrote or argued while in law school.

List the areas of law covered in any law journal article you wrote (or helped to write), or work you did as a research assistant.

List the areas of law you covered for client files in a law office, legal aid program, or pro bono program. Be as specific as possible. For students who have articled, mark down the areas of law you covered while articling. Also indicate areas of law you covered while summering or working part-time during law school. Mark with an asterisk the areas of law that you particularly enjoyed working on.

For the areas of law marked with an asterisk above, give a short reason as to why you enjoyed working on the area.

Research and Information Integration

List the articles appearing in law journals, law newspapers, and industry magazines that you read during your career search. Make a separate list of the articles you have not yet read, but would like to read. It is a good idea to clip the articles, or photocopy them, and add them to your research files for future reference.

List the career services programs and other law school programs you have attended. Make a separate list of the programs you have not yet attended but plan to attend. It is a good idea to print out or save the notice of the program because it will include the names of the speakers and where they work.

List the meetings you have had with your career services office and briefly describe the advice given at each of these meetings.

List the books and materials you have reviewed in the career services office and mark with an asterisk the books that you found particularly helpful.

Network Building

List the people you have asked for reference letters and those you would like to ask for reference letters.

List the lawyers you have met, either on your own or through a mentoring program, with whom you discussed career issues. Briefly outline their comments or suggestions. Make a separate list of the lawyers you have not yet spoken to, but would like to meet.

List the lawyers you have read about and would like to contact.

List the names of the professors with whom you would feel comfortable asking questions about practice areas and other career-related issues.

List alumni who practise in your primary areas of interest whom you would like to contact.

List family friends, neighbours, and work colleagues who may be able to answer your questions about careers.

List students in upper years, or those who are already articling, whom you would feel comfortable asking career-related questions.

Work Environment, Work Style, and Career Goals

Your work environment, work style, and career goals are important factors to consider when deciding which law offices to apply to. The following section of the workbook will help you sort out your work environment and work style preferences and your career goals. Use this section to expand your understanding of your personal values in relation to your career development. Check the applicable boxes.

Work Environment and Work Style

I prefer to work in a
- ○ small office
- ○ mid-sized office
- ○ large office

I prefer to work
- ○ near my home
- ○ downtown
- ○ in a suburb

I prefer to work in a
- ○ large city
- ○ small city
- ○ rural location

I prefer to
- ○ walk to work
- ○ commute by public transit
- ○ drive to work

I prefer to work
- ○ alone
- ○ with the same people
- ○ with different people

I prefer to have clients who are
- ○ individuals
- ○ governments or agencies
- ○ corporations

I prefer to have
- ○ the same client all the time
- ○ a few clients at a time
- ○ many different clients

I prefer to work
- ○ in an office
- ○ from home
- ○ in many locations

I would like to
- ○ work and then go home
- ○ socialize with my colleagues after hours

I prefer
- ○ to work directly with clients
- ○ to work behind the scenes
- ○ a combination of the two

I prefer to work on
- ○ one file at a time
- ○ many files at once

I prefer to practise in
- ○ one area of the law
- ○ several areas of the law

I prefer to
- ○ prepare files ahead of time
- ○ work on files that are urgent

Career Goals

I have
- ○ clear career goals
- ○ flexible career goals

I prefer to work
- ○ long hours and make a lot of money
- ○ fewer hours and live more modestly

I want to
- ○ combine my legal skills with my other skills
- ○ focus exclusively on law

I plan on
- ○ staying in law for my entire career
- ○ leaving law at the first opportunity

It is important to me to work
- ○ in a specific practice area
- ○ for a specific firm
- ○ in a specific city
- ○ does not matter

It is important to me to
- ○ effect legal/social change
- ○ make a lot of money
- ○ become well known
- ○ none of the above

Personal Values

Compared with my career, my private life is of
- ○ greater importance
- ○ equal importance
- ○ less importance

Compared with practising law, my continuing legal education (professional development) is of
- ○ greater importance
- ○ equal importance
- ○ less importance

Compared with practising law, financial matters (e.g., debt repayment, net worth, material acquisitions) are of
- ○ greater importance
- ○ equal importance
- ○ less importance

Compared to salary, benefit packages (including vacation and part-time options) are of
- ○ greater importance
- ○ equal importance
- ○ less importance

Compared to working, leisure (e.g., travel, entertainment, dining out, sports activities) is of
- ○ greater importance
- ○ equal importance
- ○ less importance

Compared to working, personal growth (e.g., spirituality, well being, mental health) is of
- ○ greater importance
- ○ equal importance
- ○ less importance

Compared to working, community involvement (e.g., volunteer work, charitable activities, PTA, clubs) is of
- ○ greater importance
- ○ equal importance
- ○ less importance

Reflect on the answers you provided and mark down what you consider your personal priorities to be. You may wish to discuss these conclusions with your career services office so that you can focus on options that match your values.

List all the adjectives and descriptors that you feel best describe your work habits and work ethic. Mark with an asterisk the four or five that you feel best describe you. If you have difficulty generating this list, consider asking a friend to describe you.

Core Messages

When you draft your cover letter and when you answer questions during your interview, it is important to develop a *thesis* about yourself. This thesis will contain core messages[1] that indicate why you are the best candidate for the position. You can develop your core messages out of the themes that emerge from your answers in your personal workbook. Core messages should be clear and supported by the information in your resumé in the academic, work, and other experience sections.

It is important to develop core messages so that you do not confuse your interviewers or overwhelm them with too much information. The reasons why you want the job and why you should be selected for the job should be contained within three or four core messages that you can refer to throughout your application process. Core messages will help to keep you organized and will help to focus the interviewer on the reasons why you are the best candidate for the position.

Here are five examples of core messages and their supporting material:

1. **Core message:** "I am an independent worker and enjoy learning through experience."
   Supporting evidence: Any work experience that demonstrates that you can work alone effectively and can learn on the job. Also, independent study programs.

2. **Core message:** "I thrive on new challenges and progress rapidly in new environments."
   Supporting evidence: Promotions in a work place (e.g., starting as a cashier and then advancing to a management position). Also, participating in and winning a mooting competition.

3. **Core message:** "I am actively involved in my academic and social communities and I am dedicated to progress and change."
   Supporting evidence: Student government, committee work, and other volunteer projects.

4. **Core message:** "I am committed to long-term projects and can focus on a single matter exclusively."
   Supporting evidence: Any long-term commitment to an activity such as remaining at the same job for many years or concentrating exclusively on one study area. Other examples include marathon running, obtaining a black belt, and grade 10 piano.

5. **Core message:** "I am accustomed to working on several projects at once and I perform well under pressure."
   Supporting evidence: Working part-time, parenting, and other commitments while studying law. Also, working in a crisis centre or involvement with other emergency programs.

---

1   I credit Derek Kent, Vice President of Veritas Communications, with introducing the term "core message" to me during a lecture he gave to Osgoode Hall Law School students in 2003.

These core messages all speak to good work habits and ethics. A core message can also be used to provide evidence of an interest in a particular practice area.

Review your personal workbook. In the left column, write down core messages that you feel apply to you. In the right column, list the supporting evidence from your work, volunteer, and academic experience. Mark with an asterisk those core messages that you believe most effectively describe you. Use these core messages to develop your cover letter and during your interview. You may find that you draw on different core messages, depending on the job you are applying for.

Core Message	Supporting Evidence

Tactical Strategies for Improvement

One of the more difficult aspects of the job search is being overlooked for a job and then having to assess what might have gone wrong. With formal recruitment programs, your interview may have been successful and the only reason you did not get the job was because there were other candidates with more experience than you. However, if you interview frequently without success, you may wish to review your interviewing style and develop strategies for improvement. This process involves close self-assessment. In order to analyze your interviewing skills in an objective manner, write down some observations about your interviewing style.

In the left column, write down the questions that you had difficulty answering during an interview. In the right column, outline a more effective answer.

Difficult Question	Improved Answer

In the left column, write down awkward or difficult experiences you had during an interview such as arriving late, extreme nervousness, forgetting the interviewer's name, stuttering during an answer, and forgetting information you put on your resumé. In the right column, list ideas for improvement. Consider discussing these experiences with your career services office and reviewing other strategies for improvement.

Difficult Situation	Improved Response

Budget

Developing a budget will help you to understand the minimum salary you will need to support yourself. Below you will find a sample budget which can be modified to suit your specific income and expense structure. In order to compare your income to your expenses, you may need to average one-time payments into monthly payments or vice versa. Once you know what your summer or articling salary will be, remember to deduct taxes, CPP, EI, and any other automatic deductions such as union dues from the gross salary. The budget below requires you to list your gross salary in the income section and to deduct your employment expenses in the expenses section. You may prefer to write your net income from your pay cheque in the income section (rather than your gross income) and omit the automatic deductions from your expenses section. The budget below is designed to be useful to you as you build your career and accumulate wealth. Your budget will probably contain many empty spaces (especially in the assets section) while you are a student.

Assets	Value
Savings account (average balance)	$
Chequing account	$
Car	$
House	$
RRSPs	$
Life insurance	$
Pensions	$
Investments	$
Collections (antiques, etc.)	$
Other _____	$
Other _____	$
Total Assets	$

Income	Monthly	Annually
Summer position	$	$
Part-time position	$	$
Full-time position	$	$
Scholarships	$	$
Bursaries	$	$
Grants	$	$
Loan #1 Amount	$	$
Loan #2 Amount	$	$
Loan #3 Amount	$	$
Gifts from parents	$	$
Other support payments/ assistance	$	$
GST and other tax refunds	$	$
Other _____	$	$
Other _____	$	$
Total Income	$	$

Expenses	Monthly	Annually
Tuition	$	$
Books and school supplies	$	$
Mortgage	$	$
Rent/condo fees	$	$
Property taxes	$	$
Home repairs and maintenance	$	$
Telephone	$	$
Cable	$	$
Internet	$	$
Hydro	$	$
Gas/Oil	$	$
Water	$	$
Public transportation/taxis	$	$
Car maintenance and gas	$	$
Car license and registration fees	$	$
Parking	$	$
Groceries and toiletries	$	$
Medical and dental (and prescriptions)	$	$
Clothing	$	$
Child care and babysitting	$	$
Pet expenses	$	$
Entertainment and dining out	$	$
Sports memberships and equipment	$	$
Other associations and memberships	$	$
Vacation and traveling	$	$
Home insurance	$	$
Car insurance	$	$
Life insurance premiums	$	$
Medical plan premiums	$	$
Payments on loan #1 including interest	$	$
Payments on loan #2 including interest	$	$
Payments on loan #3 including interest	$	$
Credit card debt	$	$
Pension payments	$	$
RRSP automatic withdrawals	$	$
Income taxes, CPP, EI etc.	$	$
Charitable contributions	$	$
Other	$	$
Other	$	$
Total Expenses	**$**	**$**

Summary	Monthly	Annually
Add Total Income	$	$
Deduct Total Expenses	($)	($)
Income to Expense Surplus or Deficit	$	$

Deadlines and Send by Dates

Remaining organized when it comes to the deadlines and the send by dates of the various recruitment programs is difficult, but essential. Use this chart to write down all the important deadlines and your own personal send by dates (i.e., dates for completing your application packages). Some examples are provided.

Program/Job	City	Application Due	Method of Delivery	Send by Date
Summer jobs	Vancouver	September 30	Hand deliver	September 28
OCIs	Toronto	September 9	School collection	September 5
Articling	Calgary	April 30	Mail	April 10
Associate Job	Windsor	June 20	E-mail to firm	June 18

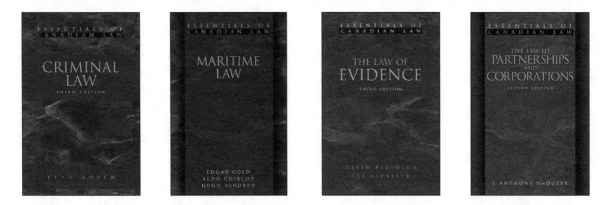